the new hermetics

the new hermetics

21st century magick for illumination and power

Jason Augustus Newcomb

Foreword by Lon Milo DuQuette

WEISER BOOKS
Boston, MA/York Beach, ME

First published in 2004 by
Red Wheel/Weiser, LLC
York Beach, ME
With offices at:
368 Congress Street
Boston, MA 02210
www.redwheelweiser.com

Library of Congress Cataloging-in-Publication Data

Newcomb, Jason Augustus.
  The new hermetics : 21st century magick for illumination and power /
Jason Augustus Newcomb ; foreword by Lon Milo DuQuette.
      p. cm.
  Includes bibliographical references.
  ISBN 1-57863-305-2
  1. Magic. 2. Hermetism. I. Title.
  BF1611.N48 2004
  135'.45--dc22

                              2004005839

Typeset in Adobe Garamond and Galahad by Jill Feron/Feron Design.
Printed in Canada
TCP

11 10 09 08 07 06 05 04
 8 7 6 5 4 3 2 1

Do what thou wilt shall be the whole of the Law.

Dedicated in service to the Interior Order and to the many adepts, ancient and modern, named and unnamed, who have made this book possible, including, in no particular order: The Master Therion, S. L. MacGregor Mathers, Allan Bennett, Helena Petrovna Blavatsky, Richard Bandler, John Grinder, Starhawk, Shakti Gawain, Edwin Steinbrecher, Israel Regardie, Milton Erickson, Julie Griffin, Janet and Stewart Farrar, Raymond Buckland, Deepak Chopra, Dion Fortune, Robert Wang, Nema, Anthony Robbins, Charles Stansfield Jones, Lia Maria Salciccia, Franz Bardon, Babaji, Tony Corinda, Robert Anton Wilson, Timothy Leary, John Lilly, Melita Denning and Osborne Philips, Donald Michael Kraig, James Wasserman, Virginia Satir, Hymenaeus Beta, Marcelo Motta, Karl Germer, Grady McMurtry, Lon Milo DuQuette, Sabazius, Robert Monroe, Carlos Castaneda, Bhagwan Shree Rajneesh, Oliver Fox, Jose Silva, Kenneth Grant, Lao Tse, Hermes Trismegistos, Scott Lesser, Peter Carroll, Phil Hine, Pan, Aiwaz, Jan Fries, Leila Waddell, Rose Crowley, L. Ron Hubbard, Plato, John Dee and Edward Kelly, Moses de Leon, Christian Rosenkreutz, Paul Foster Case, Patrick King, Karl Von Eckarthausen, Robert Hamersley, Rebecca Green, Mary Baker Eddy, George Jackson, Franz Mesmer, Paracelsus, Carl Gustav Jung, Wilhelm Reich, Leah Hirsig, Pascal Beverly Randolph, the Master Luciftias, and all the rest of you living on this plane or any other. Thank you for your wisdom and your patience. All that is worthwhile in this book I credit to your genius. All of the errors and omissions are my own.

Contents

List of Figures

List of Tables

FOREWORD

There's not the smallest orb which thou behold'st
But in his motion like an angel sings,
Still quiring to the young-ey'd cherubins;
Such harmony is in immortal souls;
But whilst this muddy vesture of decay
Doth grossly close it in, we cannot hear it.
—The Merchant of Venice, *IV, 1*

To slip the muddy vesture of decay, in which the essence of our immortal soul like a sleeping princess lies entombed, is the Great Work. It is the sacred quest of the mystic, alchemist, yogi, and magician, but it is also the inescapable destiny of every unit of evolving consciousness in the universe.

But how do we go about extricating this pristine essence from the tomb that so "grossly" closes us in? Can we chip it away like a clay cocoon? Can we shed it like a serpent's skin? Can we wash ourselves clean of it?

We can try. Indeed, plotting the escape from this prison of matter is the *raison d'être* of the world's great religions. As Hindus and Buddhists, we deny it as illusion; as Christians, we attempt to bribe our way free with a ransomed savior and, together with the other "people of the Book"—Muslims and Jews—we hate it and fear it as a devil, make war upon it as an enemy, flee from it as sin, and (discarding God-given common sense) gamble our souls on the historicity of myths and obedience to scriptural law so that, after death, we might discover we have won the prize of immortality.

Such efforts in and of themselves will remain forever doomed for, while they are effective instruments for spiritual crowd control, they ignore one very fundamental and paradoxical cosmic truth. That is, the tomb of matter, the "muddy vesture of decay," is itself an inextricable part of the essence of our immortal soul. For is it not written that the temple of initiation is also a tomb?

HERMETICS OLD AND NEW

I am particularly pleased and honored that Mr. Newcomb has asked me to pen the foreword to this remarkable book—remarkable in that it offers more than musings and the retelling of ancient material; remarkable in that he demonstrates so pleasantly that one can focus intensely upon the mystery teachings of the past without isolating oneself from the discoveries and revelations of the present, that one can unite the modern sciences of the mind with the wonder and wisdom of the ages.

It is a labor not dissimilar to the works of a number of individuals who in the twilight of the golden ages of Egypt and Greece shared their wisdom in a body of mystical texts supposedly written by the God Thoth, or Hermes, or Hermes Trismegistos. Foremost among these is one that bears the name of its mythical author, *The Emerald Tablet of Hermes*. Tradition maintains it was the first revelation of God to mankind—that it was cast in liquid emerald by the magick of alchemy, its raised letters revealing in thirteen short verses the universal operations of nature. It is the famous work that gave us the fundamental Hermetic axiom:

> *It is true and no lie, certain, and to be depended upon, that the superior agrees with the inferior, and the inferior with superior, to effect that one truly wonderful work.*[1]

Verses five and six go on to provide the diligent aspirant the mystic key by which he or she can arise from the tomb of matter even while acknowledging that the tomb is an integral part of the self.

> *The power is perfect, after it has been united with a spirituous earth. Separate the spirituous earth from the dense or crude earth by means of a gentle heat, with much attention.*[2]

It is the profoundest of cosmic ironies. The divine power, our true spiritual essence, does not achieve perfection until it hits the rock bottom of the cosmos—the dense and crude earth. It remains imperfect until the moment of entombment for the simple reason that, until that dark nadir is reached, the experiential adventure of existence remains incomplete, and self is not yet endowed with the entire spectrum of the light of consciousness—from spirit to matter, from the highest high to the lowest low.

This is why Hermetic tradition informs us that the highest angelic hosts envy the children of the dust because humans have something they will never have—a little bit of everything from top to bottom. High as they are, the angels are stuck in divine middle management without a complete stash of the raw material necessary to clone themselves to perfect godhead. Aleister Crowley describes this process as ". . . the general doctrine that the climax of the Descent into Matter is the signal for the redintegration[3] by Spirit."[4] Once the lowest low has been reached, the power is perfect and the process of return is initiated.

The Emerald Tablet of Hermes tells us how to begin. We are to "Separate the spirituous earth from the dense or crude earth by means of a gentle heat, with much attention." This doesn't mean we are to cook ourselves over a low flame (although in the symbolic language of alchemy, that's pretty much what we do). It means that through a slow, balanced, and gentle process we are (with great attention) to distill the essence of our being, the song of our soul, from the muddy vesture of decay.

This is the initiatory process of the Hermeticist old and new—a balanced and gentle program of study, practice, and meditation, mixed with the effects of one's own inherited destiny (whether you call that luck, good fortune, or karma).

Initiation is not a reward for achievement or seal of attainment. Indeed, the initiate may never attain (at least not in this incarnation). Initiation means "to begin," and the first question the candidate is asked at the threshold of the Temple is simply, "Are you ready to begin?"

Are you? If so, I can think of no better place to start than the marvelous book you hold in your hands right now—a balanced and gentle program of study, practice, and meditation. To this you must add the most important ingredient of all—yourself, the sum total of the highest high and the lowest low, your inherited destiny.

Lon Milo DuQuette
Costa Mesa, California
November 20, 2003 E.V.

INTRODUCTION

N ow that you have opened this book, I want you to know that you are beginning a wonderful and exciting journey. It is a journey inward to discover your true self and your true power. As you learn more and more about your true self, your entire life will be transformed. This book is not intended for passive consumption. It is a comprehensive instructional tool, a pathway to the evolution of human consciousness.

The New Hermetics presents a system for exploring and understanding the "magick" of what our subjective consciousness experiences. It is comprised of a group of cutting-edge spiritual technologies that systematically teach the science of illumination and power and a collection of models for looking at the unconscious mind that allow us to create a dependable system for magically changing our lives. Basically, the New Hermetics is a synthesis of Western esoteric thought, Jungian psychology, the ideas of neuro-linguistic programming, the eight-circuit model of consciousness, and Scientific Illuminism.

When you work with the New Hermetics, you experience consciousness changes that dramatically increase your ability to change your world. A young man who was working with the New Hermetics was experiencing a financial crisis. He used one of the tools that you will be taught, and the amount that he needed literally materialized in his bank account. A mysterious deposit appeared on his bank record that answered his need. This is just one example of the many surprises that are in store for you as you begin to use the New Hermetics system.

The reason that the New Hermetics works so powerfully is simple. The universe is mental. The universe is a great mind. And we are fundamentally a part of that mind. The universe is consciousness, and we are a part of that consciousness. Every thought that we have is a thought in the mind of the universe. There is no break between our individuality and the wholeness of the cosmos. The experience of separation is just a consequence, a residue of perception. This seeming separation occurs merely because we have each been given individual functions and purposes within the great cosmic mind. You do not have to believe this completely right now. But it is a key to unlocking your power, and you will hopefully come to know it as you explore the technologies of the New Hermetics. As we come to understand ourselves, we are in closer and closer relationship with the greater universal aspects of mind, and this gives us more and more power and understanding, of ourselves and everything else.

The first section of this book describes the components of the New Hermetics; the second contains the levels of the New Hermetics and the practical tools of self-discovery, transformation, and personal power. With this book, you begin your evolution into a fully self-actualized and powerful being of light. You will soon have the power to create whatever sort of wonderful life you can imagine. I congratulate you on your courage and good fortune.

In order to explore our minds with the hope of understanding the cosmic scope of our consciousness, it is necessary to have some sort of road map. Otherwise, we might quickly become lost in seas of neurotic delusion, daydreams, and fantasy. Because of this, the New Hermetics uses many of the paths drawn by modern explorers of the mind, as well as the paths trodden by the first to explore this inner landscape, the ancient magicians.

For the last two hundred years or so, we humans have been shaking off the medieval dogma of our early history and trying to come to terms with consciousness in a new way. This has resulted in many studies, explorations, and personal struggles that have nearly destroyed philosophy and certainly relegated religion into the barest of superstitious shells. However, the problem of our inner experience continues to nag us, because it seems that the human animal is by its nature a "religious creature." By this I merely mean that humans have an unquenchable need to look up to and worship strange and invisible forces that seem to guide and shape our lives. It must be remembered that science and materialism are just as invisible, mysterious, and intangible as Jehovah or Jesus.

This worship of the invisible seems inescapable. Archetypes of our highest ideals constantly inform our lives and push us in the direction they take. These archetypes take the form of gods, heroes, taboos, theories of science, and anything that we hold as being the truth, or the rules by which we lead our lives.

For centuries, we Westerners had a single explanation for all of this—the Roman Catholic Church. However, as Western societal sophistication has forced us to question the institutions of our "catholic" religion, we have turned to many alternate belief systems as a way of understanding these unconscious invisible forces. First among these was the Protestant movement that broke with the institution of the Roman Church, maintaining that a capacity for understanding religion was inherent in each individual. This revolution, along with the advent of modern science, really caused the massive atrophy of Christianity that has resulted in hundreds of separate forms of Christian belief and a host of individualistic interpretations of Christian scripture. This also resulted in a more careful examination of the Bible and a realization that, for many, the Bible does not answer their unconscious needs.

Because of this realization, in the last two centuries we have seen the wholesale importation of many Eastern philosophies that have attempted to answer these needs. For some, Eastern thought has been highly successful, but for most, these ideas are foreign and often antithetical to our basic temperaments.

In the last century, the various schools of psychology made great efforts to answer our unconscious needs. Unfortunately, psychology often tends to strip away the mystery and magick of our unconscious in an attempt to classify dysfunction and abnormality. Psychology then attempts cures of our internal ailments that merely amount to reinforcing the dominant taboos and social norms of our society. This does not in any way provide us with access to or nourishment from the source of these unconscious drives and invisible psychic forces.

However, along with the introduction of Eastern philosophy and the advent of modern psychology, there has occurred a growing revival of the ancient esoteric Western philosophies of magick. These have taken the form of neo-pagan earth spirituality movements, the rebirth of witchcraft, and the revivification of ancient Hermetic and Qabalistic practices. All of these philosophies are in essence related and intimately familiar to Westerners, because they all come from the deep recesses of the Western unconscious mind. For instance, most of us have at least some vague notions about astrology, the tarot, and the gods and myths of the Greeks and Romans. Quite simply, the New Hermetics synthesizes all of these components and more into a new system for understanding ourselves.

The word "Hermetic" is very old, indicating the studies and teachings of the preeminent Egyptian adept Hermes Trismegistos. He is often considered the emissary between humans and the gods. Hermes is also intimately related to Thoth or Tahuti, the Egyptian god of wisdom and magick (see figure 1 below).

Quite a lot of divergent material has been placed under the Hermetic banner over the centuries. However, the underlying theme of all Hermetic philosophy is that the mind shapes reality. As Hermes Trismegistos himself puts it in the *Corpus Hermeticum*, "The Mind, then, is not separated off from God's essentiality, but is united to it, as light to sun. This Mind in men is God, and for this cause some of mankind are gods, and their humanity is nigh unto divinity."[5] As I said, the key to the ancient and the new Hermetics is that the universe is mental. The universe is a great mind. The ancient Hermetic axiom, "That which is above is like that which is below to accomplish the miracle of the one thing," states the same thing in a different way. Your mind and the mind of the universe are connected inextricably to accom-

Figure 1.
Thoth or Tahuti, the
Egyptian god of magick.

plish the miracle of existence. By learning to understand your mind, you will learn to understand the universe. What's more, by learning to control your mind, you will learn to control the universe.

You must understand that, when I discuss the mind, I am not merely discussing the conscious mind as people usually think of it—the flitting thoughts about what you're going to eat for dinner or do this weekend. I am also referring to the greater aspect of mind often called today the "collective unconscious." As you become progressively more in touch with this collective unconscious, you will be increasingly able to influence the world around you. This is what the New Hermetics teaches.

I really cannot take credit for creating the New Hermetics, because it has actually been emerging slowly for the last several decades. All that I have done is to gather together the most important and life-changing aspects of many thinkers and combine them into a single cohesive, all-encompassing unit. If you'd like to see some of the names of the many modern and ancient wizards to whom I have apprenticed myself, please consult this volume's dedication and bibliography.

Specifically, the New Hermetics came into being when several modern occultists came together to practice magick as a group. Within the context of that group, several members, who also happened to be studying neuro-linguistic programming and psychologists like Carl Jung, Wilhelm Reich, and Timothy Leary, formed close associations. We realized as a group, both consciously and on an unconscious level, that by combining these modern models of consciousness and change with the ancient symbols, models, and rituals of magick, we might have something truly extraordinary. After several private and group experiments, we discovered that we had unlocked a portal with infinite possibilities. The New Hermetics was born.

What we discovered is that, by leading consciousness through certain processes, certain results always followed. Because each person is unique, the specific content of experiences may be different, but the process can be predictable and constant. We discovered that there are specific tools for directing subjective thought that cause predictable changes in consciousness and changes in the way we view ourselves. We began to transform physically, emotionally, and spiritually.

We led each other to experience out-of-body states, communion with gods and other nonhuman intelligence, and produced the experience of enlightenment and ecstasy simply by understanding that all experience is subjective.

In life, even when you are "just pretending," you are still experiencing anything that you pretend on a subjective level. To most of your brain, things that you pretend are "reality," because your brain does not differentiate between inner and outer experience. If you imagine yourself licking a lemon for long enough, your salivary glands will start to produce saliva. You can try it right now. Close your eyes and imagine yourself licking the sour inside of a lemon. You will soon begin to pucker your lips and salivate. By consciously directing your thoughts, your unconscious responds. Your brain does not differentiate between thoughts and things, because thoughts are things. The universe is mental.

On an experiential level, the more you pretend, the more real your experiences become in your mind, and the more inexplicable the practical results you will get in your exterior life. If we change things in our minds, this eventually changes things in the outer world, because it is all one thing in the end.

This realization was just the beginning of the New Hermetics. As I studied the writings of Aleister Crowley, I found that he envisioned some similar procedures and called it Scientific Illuminism. However, in the first decades of this century, he had much less information about the structure and function of the human mind than we do today. Still, he formed an elegant framework for the mystical awakening of our latent super-minds. He took the ancient Rosicrucian grades of the Hermetic Order of the Golden Dawn and provided specific meditations and mental exercises to be accomplished along a clear road of self-discovery. These procedures have been incorporated into the New Hermetics to become a system that nearly automatically transforms ordinary humans into spiritual giants.

As I began to put this together, I discovered more and more important ancient and modern practices from magicians ranging from Franz Bardon to Anthony Robbins. I have added these to the program, all the time following the direction and advice of my own "inner-planes contacts" who have guided me to this work from the beginning. What has resulted is a system that will transform you spiritually and provide you with a framework in which you can figure out your special place in the universe. This program offers you access to the awakened personal genius to accomplish anything that you can imagine. The magick of the New Hermetics is in you, in the power of your mind, which is, in the end, the cosmic mind. By following this simple program, you will awaken to your own awesome power. The New Hermetics will help you to figure out your own answers to the big questions in life: Who am I? What am I here for? Where am I going?

Many Americans and Europeans have become interested in Eastern thought and yoga. However, a lot of Eastern religion requires such incredible renunciation and behavioral restriction that it is highly impractical for the modern Westerner. What's more, the ideas do not really reflect our internal worlds. Eastern thought tends to be transcendental, ephemeral, and often insubstantial.

The West has always had a rich inner spiritual world that has admirably survived the persecution of orthodoxy. We have a beautiful set of symbols, myths, and philosophies that are unique to our collective culture. Alchemy, tarot, and astrology have always been in the background of our consciousness, waiting to be awakened by initiation into their mysteries. These Western mysteries do not require asceticism, celibacy, or behavioral restriction. In fact, they encourage us to explore our whole range of being, both divine and bestial, fully and inquisitively. We are not asked to drop out of society or to wear saffron robes or turbans or to beg in the streets. The Western mysteries are about understanding and mastering life as it is, rather than chasing ethereal chimeras into oblivion. Although they are most assuredly transcendent and evolutionary, they affirm the joy in life rather than fly from it.

The New Hermetics now makes it possible to undergo the initiation into the mysteries of consciousness and the awakening into enlightenment in a fraction of the time that was ever possible before. It systematically helps you to master your own mind in such a way that you can achieve anything and everything that you want in your life both spiritually and practically. It is a spiritual system, as well as a system of self-empowerment and personal development. In these pages, you will discover the keys to unlock the gates of heaven, and the keys to getting the most out of your life here on Earth.

As I mentioned before, our human experience is entirely subjective. Much of psychology has really missed the mark by trying to understand the human mind in objective terms. The true nature of humanity can only be understood in our subjective awareness. For this reason, people consume many more fantasy books than scientific papers. Poetry explains the soul much more succinctly than statistics. The New Hermetics is a system for understanding our subjective, spiritual nature and systematically exploring our subjective reality.

By systematically exploring the subjective process of consciousness, you will gain an ever-increasing power over your own mental process and the way that you focus on life. You will discover that, by changing your focus, you can instantly change your personal experience of life.

All mystical and occult phenomena are subjective in nature. The mystic who is drawn up into an ecstatic vision of God is having a subjective experience. This experience can easily be reproduced by systematically moving your consciousness through the same processes that the mystic goes through. Because of this understanding, what may take years for the average mystic will take just a few weeks or months for the New Hermeticist, who will also have the distinct advantage of knowing that the experience was, although beautiful and life-transforming, a subjective experience nonetheless. This will hopefully protect against the delusions of grandeur and self-importance that plague so many mystics.

The New Hermetics is also a system of magick. Magick is a tool for causing miraculous changes in the world through invisible or extraordinary means. As you awaken to your connection with universal consciousness, you will begin to gain the ability to change the universe around you. Since ancient times, this ability has been called magick. Some of the procedures described in this book are designed specifically to help you change your reality through magick. The New Hermetics contains many technologies for specifically changing your life with your awakening mental powers. These range from changing your behaviors and emotions to manifesting your desires, creating artificial elementals and talismans, and invoking archetypal forces represented by gods and other spiritual entities. All of these technologies have been broken down and simplified into their component processes and essential steps. If you follow the clear and simple procedures provided, your results are guaranteed. You will not be asked to use complicated tools or magical circles or to recite barbarous incantations. The universe is mental, and so is the magick of the New Hermetics. You will simply direct your consciousness, and results will naturally follow. You may find it valuable to act out some of the work physically, but it is not essential.

A few of the more spiritually minded among you may feel apprehensive about using your connection to the universe to manipulate reality. I assure you that there is nothing diabolical or in opposition with the universal laws about the use of magick. It is, in fact, our birthright to participate creatively in the manifestation of the universe. It is only with an understanding of and participation in the subtle, universal laws of cause and effect that we can change the world with magick. In other words, it is only by connecting and working with the universal, cosmic mind that we can do magick. Creating a change with magick is no more diabolical than building a house, planting a garden, or writing a poem. These things change the universe forever, but only within the structure of the laws of creation. There is no difference with magick.

Some people have expressed to me a fear that an unscrupulous person might use these techniques for harming or manipulating others. I assure you that those who do this give themselves all the punishment they need through the unpleasantness they wreak in their own lives. Using magick for negative purposes instantly transforms your entire world into a negative experience. For instance, if you create a talisman to injure somebody, you are instantly living in a world of negativity, in constant fear that someone may, in turn, create an injurious talisman for you. Since everyone becomes a potential black magician in your eyes, you live in a fear-based world, cut off from the universal mind that is the source of power. Your magick will begin to fail, because you are no longer in harmony with its source. If you are afraid that people are going to use magick for evil, then you are already living in this fearful world.

I would like to offer you an entirely different possibility. If you work instead to love people and to love yourself, you will quickly find yourself intimately connected to the universal mind and to your real power. This real power is harmless and yet stronger than any weapon, dwelling everywhere at the center of your being. If you live your life in this way, even those who may wish to harm you will be powerless, because you will be operating from your center. Your center is outside of the world of cause and effect, and nothing can harm it in any way.

You may want to work with a friend or partner to help guide you through some of the subjective experiences as you work through the

New Hermetics program. It is often easier to enter the proper state at first if someone acts as an assistant or coach, since almost all of the technologies of the New Hermetics require you to be in an altered state of consciousness. This state has been called the hypnagogic state, meditation, self-hypnosis, the magical trance, and many other names. It is simply an inwardly directed state of concentration and relaxation that results in greater flexibility and power of the mind. In physiological terms, the altered state is a shift into the alpha and theta ranges of brainwaves, or slowing the majority of your brainwaves down to between 3 and 15 cycles per second. This slowing down of the brainwaves allows for the introspection, "peak experiences," and "oceanic consciousness" that connect us with our unconscious powers and resources. It is sometimes a confusing space at first; so working with someone else may make things easier. It is not required by any means. Extremely deep states of consciousness are not really even necessary for the majority of the tools in this book. Simply being relaxed and focused is the only requirement. If you invest a little bit of energy and time, the possibilities for your development are unlimited. You can also obtain audio programs for all of the New Hermetics tools at *www.newhermetics.com*.

The New Hermetics has ten levels of instruction that correspond to the ten grades of the ancient Rosicrucian brotherhood. The names of the levels have been modernized to shake off the last dusty vestiges of Victorian melodrama from the very real and powerful process of initiation and spiritual evolution. Each of the levels of the New Hermetics introduces us to greater and greater internal resources that allow us to evolve with incredible speed and precision. They are as follows:

1. **Initiate**—Earth, mastery of behavior and visualization in the aethyr.
2. **Zealot**—Water, mastery of emotions, breathing and aethyric energy.
3. **Practitioner**—Air, mastery of mind, beliefs and projecting aethyric energy.
4. **Philosopher**—Fire, mastering creativity, values, directing aethyric energy.
5. **Adept**—Spirit, development of relationship with cosmic consciousness.

6. **Advanced Adept**—Power to direct forces of cosmic consciousness.
7. **Perfect Adept**—Wisdom and ability to share these forces with others.
8. **Master**—Mastery of cosmic consciousness.
9. **Mage**—Mastery of universal power.
10. **Ultimate Master**—Mastery of universal self.

Part I

THE NEW
HERMETICS
PROGRAM

CHAPTER 1

BECOMING A
NEW HERMETICIST

I n essence, the New Hermetics is a system for getting in touch with
cosmic, universal consciousness, and eventually experiencing transcendental, ecstatic union with this consciousness. By this I mean a
personal and transformational link with the source of consciousness,
the creative intelligence that forms the universe. Throughout history,
this has been called "union with God." However, the New Hermetics is
not based on any particular theory about religion, or the nature of God
or the universe. Rather it is based on the methods that humans have
used since the beginning of time to establish a connection with their
source. These methods form the process of exploring our internal worlds
and ourselves until we eventually discover our center, the source of our
consciousness itself.

Because of this, people from any background can enjoy the benefits of the New Hermetics in their lives. All that is required is an open
mind and an open heart. These need not even be developed in full,
because the methods of the New Hermetics will greatly assist you in
opening both of these organs. It is not necessary for you to believe in
God in any traditional sense or to disbelieve in God. It is not necessary for you to accept or reject any religious inclinations that you may
or may not have. The New Hermetics will give you the opportunity

to experience universal consciousness or God freely, in exactly the way that is appropriate for you.

The magical and mystical quest for enlightenment is an entirely personal and intimate journey. I cannot say for certain what your enlightenment will be like, any more than you can for me. The wonderful thing about the New Hermetics is that it is entirely based on process rather than dogma, so you will be free to experience your personal illumination in exactly the manner that is correct for you.

In order to become a New Hermeticist, you must adopt several new models of behavior. These will help you to actualize your powers in the fullest and most helpful and positive way possible. You are about to go into uncharted territory, and without these guideposts, it is easy to become lost in the morass of your own fears, illusions, and bad habits. We are all limited beings, and even our most profound insights are limited by our human imperfections. At our best, we are reflections of our ideals, but to mistake ourselves for these ideals is the first error of the mystic.

The basic guideposts of the New Hermeticist are simple: cultivate a natural cheerful skepticism, a sense of possibility, knowledge that truth is entirely subjective, an awareness and cultivation of the basic mystical states, and an endless pursuit of equilibrium.

SKEPTICISM[6]

The first requirement of the would-be New Hermeticist is a probing skepticism toward the whole project. By skepticism, I mean the behavior of questioning and thoroughly investigating all things before believing them. I do not mean approaching your investigation with a bias toward doubt, which can be ruinous. The true skeptic is neither credulous nor incredulous. Don't take my word for anything. Investigate every statement I make. You are the only arbiter of truth that has any validity in your universe.

Blind dogma must be rooted out of your mind completely. If you are a Baptist Christian, by all means you may continue to be one, but if you experience something outside of the limits of the letters of that faith, do not be too quick to dismiss it. If you are a scientific atheist, you may feel free to follow your inclinations, but don't be surprised if you must expand your horizons as your adventure takes you into wild new territory. Adhering rigidly to any limited concept of the universe will only serve to distort your own perceptions. Human beings, by their nature, seem to long for something to believe and there is real danger in that desire. Whether the belief is in some traditional form of Christianity, Judaism, or other faith or in a dogmatic, scientific materialism, the result is the same. Your outlook will be limited and restricted within that bubble.

And please don't confuse skepticism with laziness. As you begin to explore this system, you may ask yourself questions like, "What's the point of that?" or, "What's he trying to make me do that for?" or, "I don't think this is going to work at all." These questions do not necessarily constitute skepticism. They may merely be the tools of sloth trying to avoid any kind of true exploration. Eagerness, intentness, concentration, vigilance—these are the qualities required of a skeptic. Both the skeptic and the lazy fool may ask questions, but the skeptic begins to search for a real answer, while the fool uses the question to avoid doing anything.

When the light of illumination dawns and you experience your union with cosmic, universal consciousness, as a skeptic you will not accept this ecstatic vision as "truth" and begin to preach from the mountaintops. You will continue to question, continue to search, and that search will never end. My own search continues to this day and will continue forever.

POSSIBILITY

Once you have grasped the importance of skepticism, you are confronted with a seeming paradox. In order to take advantage of the mental technology of the New Hermetics, you must explore territories that may seem, on the surface, unbelievable. You will become acquainted with an unfamiliar cosmology. You will explore seemingly imaginary things like internal energy centers, invisible life forces, gods, angels, and elemental beings. This cosmology may or may not have any scientific or physiological validity. This will give pause to your skeptical nature, and you will naturally insist upon an explanation.

The simple fact is that these inner-world phenomena have experiential validity. If you concentrate on your third eye, the space on your forehead between your eyes, within a very few minutes you will note a slight tingling sensation. You may close this book for a moment and experiment right now. Concentrate for a few minutes on this spot between your eyes.

If you really just closed your eyes and concentrated, you discovered some strange sensations coming from this area. The New Hermetics calls this an "energy center" only because that is the most convenient way to describe it, if you hope to get anything out of it. It could just as easily be called a fantasy, but that wouldn't really take us very far. However, you must also avoid falling into the trap of believing that this truly is an "energy center."

The only thing you must maintain is a fierce, ever-questioning desire for knowledge, and an endless sense of possibility. There may come a time when you will accept as fact the existence of energy centers, spirits, and invisible worlds beyond the physical. When performing the New Hermetics program, these phenomena are necessary for the process, because they lead us inward and give us places to hang our experiences. But there is really no reason to attach any philosophical importance to any of it. Self-actualization is the goal, not religious or philosophical conversion.

TRUTH

Truth is a subjective experience. Is there even such a thing as objective reality? Objective reality is by far the most improbable of all of humankind's abstract ideas. In order for anything to be objectively real, it must be able to be isolated from any context and still be itself. Comparison of any kind would then be impossible, because all methods of doing so would be removed in the process. Once you place anything into a context, it loses every drop of its objectivity, becoming simply another subjective quantity in the palette of your existence.

Take, for example, an apple. The first time you see an apple, you instantly notice a million things about it. To each of these observations you attach different degrees of importance. These simple observations place the apple completely outside the realm of objectivity. All of your further relations with that apple are in the context of those opinions. If the observations match past observations that please your aesthetic sense, you may eat the apple. If not, the apple may be avoided. Either way, the apple does not exist except within the context of your opinion. There is no way to objectively view it. The same may also be said of the qualities that are observed. The color, shape, texture, and smell of the apple only exist in the context of your experiences with those qualities. This can be extended forever.

The same also holds true for mathematics and the physical sciences. The number 2 is only meaningful in the context of 1 and 3. Without a context, 2 is simply a meaningless glyph formed with ink on a piece of paper. A star is only big and bright when compared to something that is smaller and more dull.

To say that any idea is more real or true than any other idea, while fair from the perspective of subjectivity, is a completely meaningless statement. Nothing in this universe is real, and nothing is unreal. There is no correct answer to any question, because both question and answer are subjective. "Is the sky blue?" This simple question has no clear answer. While it may appear blue to the eye, it is not blue at all. Its apparent blueness is the result of the relations between our atmosphere and blue light waves. The sky is anything but blue. From a poetical perspective, it is many colors, reflecting the mood of the ever-changing human spirit. After all, it is violet and orange when romance fills our souls, golden at the dawn, and black when our hearts are low. Moreover, all of this is subject to an infinite number of interpretations.

It is from this standpoint that you must approach the mysteries of the universe. You can never really hold onto any idea as being true. Instead, you must merely decide which ideas are useful at the moment for your purposes, and be ready to cast them aside as soon as they are no longer necessary.

MYSTICAL STATES

Mystical states are experiences that are outside of normal reality. They are inwardly directed experiences that can be colorful, wonderful, and usually transformative. There are many different mystical states, corresponding to the depth of our state of consciousness. The deeper we travel within, the more profound our mystical experiences tend to be. There are, in fact, five or more distinct phases in the evolution of mystical phenomena.[7] The first five levels of the New Hermetics systematically introduce you to these phases.

Phase 1: Internal Images—The Aethyr

The first stage of your internal mystic awareness is the pictures, sounds, and sensations that you experience when you close your eyes. These experiences have been called the astral plane, the astral light, or the ethereal plane. I have chosen to call this area of awareness the aethyr, which I think to be the most elegant of its names. The images in the aethyr are usually shadowy and meaningless, comprised of the dreams and memories that pop into your mind. These are often random images that intrude upon you, as well as images you call up when visualizing, daydreaming, or meditating. This phase is marked by the appearance of all sorts of astral creatures, which you may begin to see even with your eyes open. There are infinite shapes and beings that you can and will see. These shadowy forms are not particularly important in and of themselves. They will be easily observed with the techniques of astral travel and visualization that are explained in the Initiate level of training. In the Initiate level, you will learn to master these images and create them at will.

Phase 2: Sensual Images—The Emotional World

The second phase of mystical awareness is your emotional world. You will explore this phase in the Zealot level of New Hermetics training. In this phase, you become intimately aware of your internal experiences, your feelings, and your processes of emotion. This phase is often marked by astral or aethyric visions accompanied by strong emotional feelings, or mystical energy. As you explore your body's energy centers, you may unlock all kinds of emotional experiences. You may even experience visions of godlike beings or other archetypal figures that produce euphoric states. You can also experience formless emotional ecstasies and visions of beauty and harmony at this phase. The emotional exercises and the archetypal explorations in the second part of this book will introduce you to this phase.

Phase 3: Intellectual Symbols and Concepts—The Mental World

The third stage of the internal mystical process is the mental or intellectual world. It is the world of symbols and systems. You will explore this phase in the Practitioner level of New Hermetics training. This phase of mystical experience is marked by formless experiences that may be pure symbols or ideas. Although intellectual in nature, the states of consciousness in this stage are subtle enough that your rational mind may not really understand them. This is marked by an experience of knowing something important, but not really understanding how to express it or even how to think about it. The consciousness-expansion exercise and the belief-changing exercises answer to this mystical phase to some degree.

Phase 4: Awareness of Self as Self—The Causal World

In the fourth phase, you will begin to gain a sense of the entire universe as one thing that you fundamentally are on all levels. You will explore this phase in the Philosopher level of New Hermetics training. At this stage, you will begin to understand yourself to be intimately connected with and in a greater sense identical with everything. More simply, you begin to gain access to the collective unconscious and begin to realize your identity within it. The practices of Supercharging Your Intuition and Rising on the Planes, as well as Invoking the Gods awaken the states of consciousness associated with this phase.

Phase 5: Cosmic Awareness, Enlightenment, Illumination

This phase is pure consciousness. Your consciousness slips into the gap between your thoughts, "stopping the world." You move into a state in which all becomes one, without differentiation, and disappears beyond comprehension. This is the state of bliss known as *samadhi* to the yogis. In the West, it has been called "The Knowledge and Conversation of Your Holy Guardian Angel," "illumination," or "union with God." The practice Conscious Communication with Cosmic Consciousness is the main New Hermetics tool for this experience, but many of the tools in this book may result in this state if you are willing and able to experience it. You will explore this phase in the Adept level of New Hermetics training. My first book, *21st Century Mage*, offers many alternative methods for experiencing this transcendental consciousness.

There are actually many further developments of the mystical phenomena, but they are in the realm of Mastery and are beyond the scope of this book. As a New Hermetics Master, you may find these further states of refined bliss and states beyond bliss if and when you are ready.

EQUILIBRIUM

As you begin this inward path to illumination, the single most important instruction is to strive constantly to establish equilibrium in yourself. Before the Temple of King Solomon there stood two pillars, equal in size, to demonstrate this fact. These pillars represent the polarity of the universe. In other cultures, these have been represented as yin and yang, Shiva and Shakti, and many other words and ideas. You must remember that the sum of two equal and opposite forces is zero. All forces in the universe demand this balance of zero, and this is, of course, the basis for the Newtonian axiom that every action is followed by an equal and opposite reaction. When imbalance occurs, nature seeks to rectify the disparity with cold precision.

However, change, evolution, and progress can only occur in imbalance. Any action, at least temporarily, must destroy equilibrium. Therefore, you must balance every experience with its equal and opposite. It is only then that both progress and equilibrium can coexist. An unbalanced approach to anything will only end in the universe demanding its toll, and this most often results in catastrophe. I wish I had more fully understood this concept when I began my own work.

Traditional morality argues that some things are right, and others wrong. Moralists claim that some people are good, and others bad. These weighted terms are in fact ridiculous and in direct contradiction to nature. Morality has no real place at all in the life of the true mystic. Without the Satanist, the evangelist would be out of a job, having nothing to denounce. Without the evangelist, the Satanist would have nothing to rebel against, and would quickly tire of wearing so much black. Morality is entirely subjective. There is nothing that should be denied, disregarded, or shunned. All of your being must be explored. All of your being must be balanced to perfection.

The truth of illumination is beyond the capabilities of the rational mind to understand. Every rational statement contains a contradiction.

Discover the contradiction in every situation. Seek to balance every part of your being and personality, and spiritual light will then dawn inside of you. Equilibrium is key.

THE MODELS AND TOOLS OF THE NEW HERMETICS

Hermeticism has always been a syncretistic and eclectic system of ideas that draws to itself anything and everything that is useful for the creation of greater awareness and power. Ancient Hermeticism was perhaps at its height in the days of Alexandria when trading and imperialism drew together many vastly different cultures that shared their secrets and tools for magick and mysticism in the cosmopolitan atmosphere of the ancient city. It was here that Hermeticism drew to itself the most interesting and powerful magical formulas and philosophies. The New Hermetics has inherited this synthesizing nature, and anything and everything that we think might be useful has been drawn into the system to create a complete and comprehensive scientific system for wisdom and power.

There are many elements that make up the models and tools of the New Hermetics. This is only the barest sketch of the contributing models and tools. In the next few chapters, I will attempt to more fully elucidate their contributions to the New Hermetics.

The key source for the New Hermetics is, of course, the ancient Hermetics. From it we draw many of the fundamental models that the system relies on. Most important, the ancient Hermetics provides us with the idea of the universe as an intelligence that is related intimately with our own intelligence. The idea that the universe is a great mind is the entire platform upon which the New Hermetics is built. Also, we draw from Hermeticism the ideas of the four ancient elements with their unique psychology and powers, as well as the sacred use of numbers and geometry. From the ancient Hermetics also come the principles of alchemy, the planetary influences, and astrology, which play subtle but important roles in the New Hermetics.

Of almost equal importance to the New Hermetics are the Qabala and its pictorial key, the tarot. The Qabala is an ancient Hebrew mystical system that played a huge part in medieval magick and metaphysics. It is from the Qabala that the New Hermetics system of levels derives. The

Rosicrucian grade system is based directly on the ten *sephiroth* of the Qabalistic Tree of Life, and the levels of New Hermetics training depend wholly on this system. The whole sephirothic system is really the backbone of the New Hermetics, and every one of the tools can be more clearly understood by placing it within the context of the Tree of Life. For instance, the five mystical states described above correspond to the lower five sephiroth on the Tree. What's more, every symbol, archetype, and New Hermetics exercise has a specific place on the Tree of Life. The whole system begins to coalesce as you begin to understand the figure of the Tree. This will all be explained more clearly in an upcoming chapter.

The main mystical tools of the New Hermetics derive from Scientific Illuminism, which was an attempt on the part of Aleister Crowley and several other adepts of the Hermetic Order of the Golden Dawn to create a pure system of mysticism and magick, without the dogma and ceremonial clap-trap of earlier occult groups. The New Hermetics has further reduced these practices to their pure essences and turned the tools of Scientific Illuminism into a simple series of practical methods for attainment.

This distillation has only been possible through the use of modeling techniques from the cutting edge technology of neuro-linguistic programming (NLP). NLP is the study of subjective consciousness and contains a large body of tools for learning about and changing consciousness. From NLP, we borrowed several tools for changing states, beliefs, and meta-programs, as well as NLP ideas about representational systems, reframing, and anchors.

Several modern psychologists have also informed the New Hermetics. From the work of C. G. Jung, we have obtained a clear view of the "collective unconscious" of humanity and this has made it possible for us to begin the process of really understanding the components of the path of initiation from the inside. From Wilhelm Reich, we have drawn several important understandings about the "life energy" (orgone) that gets trapped and poisoned in our "body armor," preventing us from really getting the most out of life. From the truly avant-garde psychologist Timothy Leary, we have borrowed the "eight-circuit model of consciousness," which we have found to provide truly profound insights into human nature, Qabala, and the driving structure of the human animal.

We have also borrowed a few elements from the spiritual teachings of the East—a few breathing exercises, mental concentration practices, and the ideas about energy centers or *chakras*. As you can see, a huge amount of information from many different sources has been gathered together succinctly in these pages to create a complete schema for the illumination of the soul into enlightenment and power over all areas of life.

As you study this book, you will discover many parallels between these various ideas and between symbols from among the various models and tools. We call these correspondences, and there is something very important that must be understood immediately about these correspondences. A correspondence means that there is a meaningful relationship between two ideas. It does not mean that they are identical. If I tell you that there is a correspondence between the element earth, the sephirah Malkuth, the alchemical principle of salt, the kinesthetic sense, and Timothy Leary's first bio-circuit, this means that I believe that all of these concepts share relationships. They are not all the same thing. Likewise, we can say that the goddesses Astarte and Isis share many correspondences, but it would be a terrible error to assume that they are the same goddess. Also, the Sun and gold are said to correspond to each other, but to say that the Sun is gold or gold is the Sun is very silly. If you keep this in mind, you will find your life much easier. Now, let's discuss some of these models of the New Hermetics in a little more detail.

CHAPTER 2

ANCIENT MODELS FOR THE NEW HERMETICS

The original Hermetic adepts had a double heritage. The Hermetic school was really a Greek synthesis of the earlier Egyptian mystery schools. Hermes is the Greek form of the Egyptian God Tahuti or Thoth. He is the god of wisdom and magick. The relationships between and history of Greek and Egyptian mystery schools are complex, lost in prehistory, and far beyond the scope of this book. However, in the first few years of our common era, Hermetic magick was at its height. Many differing streams were brought together, among them the Gnostics, the Neoplatonists (who were derived themselves from the earlier teachings of Plato, Socrates, and Pythagoras), the Jewish Qabalists, alchemists, such influential magician-philosophers as Apollonius of Tyana, Apuleius of Maduara, and many others. We have drawn out some of the essentials of these philosophies and incorporated them into the heart of the New Hermetics.

SELF-MASTERY

It is said that inscribed above the gates to the ancient temples of mystery were the words, "Know Thyself." Socrates, too, emphasized these words as the touchstone of personal development. This is really the fundamental principle of the New Hermetics. The whole purpose behind any initiatory structure is to lead you as an initiate to a greater understanding of yourself. This understanding then translates into the ability to act consistently and congruently in accordance with your own true will.

By understanding ourselves, we come to understand the purpose of our existence, and with that purpose clearly in mind, we can accomplish anything. As you go through the exercises of the New Hermetics, you will systematically begin to know yourself more clearly than ever before. With that knowledge will come the ability to understand life more clearly and the ability to change your life in any way.

By understanding yourself and the forces of life, you will also begin to understand the universe more clearly.

MACROCOSM AND MICROCOSM

The Emerald Tablet of Hermes Trismegistos begins with these words: "Certain, 'tis true and without doubt, that which is above is like that which is below to accomplish the miracle of the one thing." This simple statement tells us explicitly that humans are a reflection of the entire universe. We are a microcosm of the universal macrocosm. Inside us is a complete universe. This is our personal universe, but it is "like unto" the universe above and outside of ourselves. In the end, there is little difference between these two. By understanding this concept, we can begin to understand our awesome power and responsibility. When we think a thought or create a picture in our minds, a corresponding picture is created in the macrocosm. So, if we continually think limiting, negative thoughts, then we have limited negative experiences in the world. However, if we begin to think positive, enriching thoughts that contain unlimited possibilities, then the whole range of universal power opens up to us.

What's more, as we begin to really know our own internal nature, we find that we are actually discovering the nature of the universe. The potential for our development is unlimited. All that it takes is a willingness to explore ourselves. There is a catch, however. Our potential power and possibility is virtually unlimited, but it is limited practically by our beliefs and our own patterns of thought. For example, if we want to bring about world peace, we can think the thought "world peace, world peace, world peace" over and over in our minds. Then when we open our eyes, to our dismay, we find that the world is not at peace. The reason for this is simple. We do not believe that we are making a change with this thought. Not really. At a deep layer of the mind, we are thinking, "But this won't work, the world is too big for me to control. There's too much hate . . . etc." and this guarantees the failure of our conscious thought projection out into the macrocosm. However, as you begin to really understand your mind and alter some of your fundamental limiting beliefs, you will find that your thoughts really are things and that they do influence the world. Who knows, perhaps some day you will open your eyes and find that the world really is at peace. After all, peace can only begin inside each of us.

The Four Elements

The ancient Greek philosophers saw the world in terms of four elements: fire, water, air, and earth. These elements were not the literal things themselves, but poetic expressions of the ideal qualities of these things. Nearly everything could be classified by its nature as related to

Symbol	Element	Characteristics
△	**Fire**	warmness and dryness, and the quality of expansion
▽	**Water**	coldness and wetness, and the quality of contraction or shrinking
△	**Air**	warmness and moistness, and the quality of lightness
▽	**Earth**	coldness and dryness, and the quality of heaviness

Table 1. The four elements and their characteristics.

Figure 2. The four elements combined with spirit.

these four elements. The four elements contained the essential natures of everything in existence. Their qualities are shown in Table 1 (see page 29).

These four elements were said to be accompanied by a fifth element, spirit, or aethyr, which was said to hold them together and combine them, but always retaining their individual character (see figure 2 above).

Everything was made up of combinations of these elements. Of course, modern science has found other explanations for the physical world, but the ancient elements still play an important role in our psychology and in our spirit. The element of earth can be considered the animal needs of the human mind; the element of water, the emotions; the element of air, the intellect; and the element of fire, the will. It will later be seen that there is a strong correspondence between this and the first four bio-circuits of Timothy Leary's eight-circuit model of consciousness.

The first four levels of the New Hermetics largely introduce us to these four elements as spiritual models and teach us how to use these models effectively to help us understand and creatively change the way that we behave and think. You will learn how to re-engineer or reframe the way that you feel about all aspects of your life in order to maximize your personal pleasure and power.

Also, the four elements correspond to tendencies in our personalities. By balancing these tendencies, we can achieve a greater level of personal equilibrium. In ancient times, these elemental personality types were called the four humors: phlegmatic, choleric, melancholic, and sanguine. As you look at Figure 3 (below), you can see that you have certain positive and negative character tendencies that correspond to the elements.

You will notice that right now you tend toward one or two of the elements more than the others. This represents an imbalance in your personality. What's more, for every positive quality, you undoubtedly possess the negative quality corresponding to it. You at least have the potential for these negative qualities in some small degree. In the New Hermetics program, you will redress these imbalances and fully actualize all of the positive elemental qualities in yourself. There are, of course,

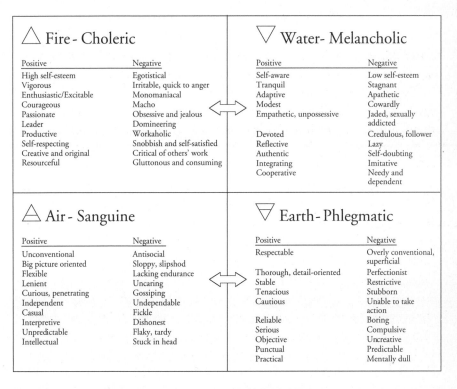

△ Fire - Choleric

Positive	Negative
High self-esteem	Egotistical
Vigorous	Irritable, quick to anger
Enthusiastic/Excitable	Monomaniacal
Courageous	Macho
Passionate	Obsessive and jealous
Leader	Domineering
Productive	Workaholic
Self-respecting	Snobbish and self-satisfied
Creative and original	Critical of others' work
Resourceful	Gluttonous and consuming

▽ Water- Melancholic

Positive	Negative
Self-aware	Low self-esteem
Tranquil	Stagnant
Adaptive	Apathetic
Modest	Cowardly
Empathetic, unpossessive	Jaded, sexually addicted
Devoted	Credulous, follower
Reflective	Lazy
Authentic	Self-doubting
Integrating	Imitative
Cooperative	Needy and dependent

△ Air - Sanguine

Positive	Negative
Unconventional	Antisocial
Big picture oriented	Sloppy, slipshod
Flexible	Lacking endurance
Lenient	Uncaring
Curious, penetrating	Gossiping
Independent	Undependable
Casual	Fickle
Interpretive	Dishonest
Unpredictable	Flaky, tardy
Intellectual	Stuck in head

▽ Earth- Phlegmatic

Positive	Negative
Respectable	Overly conventional, superficial
Thorough, detail-oriented	Perfectionist
Stable	Restrictive
Tenacious	Stubborn
Cautious	Unable to take action
Reliable	Boring
Serious	Compulsive
Objective	Uncreative
Punctual	Predictable
Practical	Mentally dull

Figure 3. Positive and negative characteristics of the humors and their corresponding elements.

many other character traits that I have not included here, but these lists should give you an impression of each element.

The four elements also correspond to the four suits in the tarot:

Fire............Wands
Water ....Cups
Air.............Swords
Earth ....Pentacles

Moreover, they correspond to the four worlds and parts of the soul in the Qabala, which we will explore briefly in the next section. Suffice it to say that the four ancient elements are some of the most important spiritual building blocks of the entire New Hermetics.

SACRED NUMBERS AND GEOMETRY

I will touch only momentarily on this point here, but the idea that numbers and shapes have special, spiritual meanings is very important to the New Hermetics, because it is one of the organizing principles we will use to prepare our minds to create change. Numbers have always been considered sacred, and special numbers are frequently incorporated into the architecture of ancient temples and holy places. Basically, we will concern ourselves primarily with the *decad*, or numbers one through ten. The sacred meanings of numbers have been interpreted since the time of Pythagoras and before in many different ways. For the sake of simplicity and consistency, our use of numbers will be confined to a few simple Qabalistic interpretations. Table 2 (opposite) gives a summary of these interpretations, along with planetary and geometric correspondences.

This may all seem confusing or superfluous, but you will come to understand over the course of your work that, by understanding the internal nature of these numbers, you can understand by analogy your own internal nature. By using these correspondences, you can literally change your relationship with the universe. By understanding numbers and their corresponding shapes, you can contact the interior meanings beneath the surface of number and transform your life in unimaginable ways. It will all become much clearer as we progress.

Number	Spiritual Correspondence	Astrological Correspondence	Psychological Correspondence	Geometric Correspondence
1.	Unity, beingness itself, the self of deity, beyond Fatherhood and Motherhood	Universe as singularity	Highest spirit	Point
2.	Father, the divine will, the word, Logos, action, expansion	Zodiac	Creative self	Line
3.	Mother, matter, the divine intelligence, Sophia, an arena for action, structure, limitation	Saturn	Intuitive self	Triangle
4.	The solid of matter existing in time, mercy, authority, generosity, leadership	Jupiter	Memory	Quadrangle
5.	The interplay of the divine will with matter, force, motion, energy, justice, force, violence	Mars	Will	Pentagram or pentangle
6.	The Son, divine mind, harmony	Sun	Imagination	Hexagram or hexangle
7.	The attraction of forces, gravity, divine desire	Venus	Desire	Septagram
8.	The laws of the universal structure, mathematics, physics, divine reason	Mercury	Reason	Octagram
9.	Stability in change, the astral or aethyric matrix	Moon	Subconscious	Enneagram
10.	The Daughter, the physical universe	Earth	Physicality	Decagram

Table 2. The decad and its correspondences.

ALCHEMY

From ancient alchemy, we draw three very important alchemical principles: sulphur, mercury, and salt. Like the four elements, these principles are not the physical things themselves, but qualities that these substances represent. However, as Table 3 shows (see page 34), while the four elements relate to structure, the three principles relate to movement and state.

Symbol	Principle	Energy
🜍	**Sulphur**	energetic, expansive movement, metabolism, destruction, dissolution, evaporation
☿	**Mercury**	fluid, changing movement, inconsistency and integration, balancing salt and sulphur
🜔	**Salt**	slow, heavy movement, stability, solidification, crystallization, condensation

Table 3. The alchemical principles and their energies.

All of us move through these principles in the way that we process and interact with the world, as shown in Figure 4 (below).

Alchemy has also given us important insight into ourselves through its study of metals. Again, these metals are not the physical things, but qualities or parts of the human and divine mind. The alchemical metals correspond to the seven ancient planets. In fact, our modern symbols for the planets are just the ancient alchemical symbols for the metals in correspondence with the planets. In Table 4 (opposite), notice that the numbers relate to the numbers of the decad and their planetary correspondences shown in Table 2 (see page 33).

These seven metals and planets represent qualities or parts in our minds that are either expressed or unexpressed. Often, we do not allow ourselves to awaken these planetary energies fully in ourselves. For instance, many people find it very easy to express the Mercuric, logical parts of themselves, but find it impossible to communicate their emotional, lunar parts. Others find it easy to be thoughtful and generous, Jupiterean, but find it impossible to express the Martial strength to say no. Through the practices of the New Hermetics, you will begin to connect fully with these abstract qualities in yourself. Through the processes of invocation and integration, you will

Figure 4. The alchemical principles as a process of interaction with the world.

Number	Symbol	Metal	Planet	Correspondence
3	♄	Lead	Saturn	Structure, limitation, seriousness, responsibility
4	♃	Tin	Jupiter	Generosity, abundance, leadership, vision
5	♂	Iron	Mars	Justice, strength, force, violence
6	☼	Gold	Sun	Beauty, harmony, balance, wholeness
7	♀	Copper	Venus	Love, passion, aesthetics, nurture
8	☿	Mercury	Mercury	Reason, communication, logic, knowledge
9	☾	Silver	Moon	Imagination, instinct, subconscious, emotion

Table 4. Alchemical metals and their correspondences.

learn how to awaken the positive aspects of these qualities in yourself and to pacify the negative parts of these qualities.

It is important to remember and understand that all of these tables and figures are just models, convenient methods of organizing our internal nature to understand ourselves more clearly and give us a systematic way to approach positive change. They do not necessarily represent facts of nature and are subject to the limitations created by any model.

GNOSIS

Several ancient religions were categorized as "gnostic." Many of them had entirely different views about the universe, and we will not dwell on these differences here. The most important fundamental of the Gnostic cosmology is that the God that people generally worship, the god of the world, is an evil *demiurge*. Behind the god of the world is a god of pure light, considered by the Gnostics to be the real God. In the New Hermetics, this translates to the idea that our true inner selves are quite different from the selves that we express to the world. Behind the veil of our neuroses and patterns of behavior our real selves live, quietly waiting to be set free.

The Gnostics held that most people mistakenly worshipped the god of form, who was the creator of the physical world of forms, but not the true god. This god of form was evil, because, in the physical world, there is suffering and pain. Most of us experience a similar psychological condition when we mistake our neuroses and conditioned responses for our real inner selves. Most of us think that our conditioned responses to life are "the real us." This couldn't be further from the truth. The way that you react to your experiences in life is really just a set of routines. You may think that these routines are your own unique personality, but they're mostly imitated from other people. You imitate your parents, your friends, your enemies, and your lovers. Have you noticed yourself saying some distinctive phrase or using some particular gesture that your current sexual partner uses? That's just a simple routine you've picked up to feel closer to your partner. There isn't very much unique about any of our behaviors. That's because our behaviors are not "us." They are merely our attempts to fit in with the people around us. The real "us" is always hidden away, deep inside. If you think about this for even a moment, you will know that what I'm saying is true.

The way that the Gnostics sought to approach their true selves, and the true God, was through *gnosis*, transcendental, spiritual knowledge. The New Hermetics teaches that gnosis and mystical illumination are one and the same phenomenon. Through the New Hermetics, you will learn to connect with this real you and express whatever part of that real you you want to express.

QABALA AND TAROT

Many have called the Qabala the yoga of the West. Qabala is the ancient mystical tradition of Israel. Alongside the Jewish tradition there developed an Hermetic Qabala that combined the rich Hermetic symbology with the Hebrew philosophy and the all-important glyph of the Qabala, the Tree of Life. Over the past few centuries, tarot cards have become a visible and pictorial portrait of many of the most important Hermetic and Qabalistic concepts.[8] It is with the tarot-related aspect of the Qabala, with its rich archetypal imagery and spiritual truth, that the New Hermetics is most concerned.

In the tarot, the numbered cards of the Minor Arcana represent the ten sephiroth or divine emanations. The four suits represent the four Qabalistic worlds and the four elements. The twenty-two letters of the Hebrew alphabet or paths are represented by the twenty-two Major Arcana, or trump cards. The court cards—King, Queen, Prince, and

Page or Princess—represent the power of the divine Tetragrammaton in the four worlds. I will explain these terms as we go along, but we are not going to dwell at length on these things here. What are really important are the archetypes that these symbolic pictures evoke. These are the mystical energies that we will work with in the New Hermetics.

For the New Hermetics, the Qabala is the paradigm on which the whole system of initiation is based. The Qabala is a pattern that represents the process of creation from the singularity of universal cosmic unity, consciousness (also known as God), to the myriad forms of the physical universe. The Qabala is a descriptive model for understanding the unfoldment of spirit into matter. The most important symbol of the Qabala, and really the synthesis of the whole system, is the Tree of Life (see figure 5, page 38).

The Ten Sephiroth

The ten spheres in Figure 5, called *sephiroth* in Hebrew, represent divine emanations, or levels in the manifestation of creation. These emanations represent the evolution of the universe from the single thought of divine intelligence to the myriad forms of physical reality. This ten-fold evolution is a very complete representation of the subtle development of reality.

The Tree of Life is merely a model, but it is very complete and practical. It is a paradigm for looking at abstract ideas, and should not be confused with truth. You will see that we can place many different constructs conveniently into this ten-fold division of the universe.

In Table 5 (see page 39), I've placed the numbers and names of the sephiroth, along with their planetary attributions and brief interpretations, so that you can really begin to put all this together. If you look back to Table 2 (see page 33), you will notice that this evolution has also been explained there.

These energies can be seen in the numbered tarot cards. The archetypal energies of these symbolic emanations of divinity have been represented as gods in many cultures. By understanding these archetypal energies, you can really begin to understand the collective unconscious described by Jung. Table 6 (see page 39) gives a brief overview of this comparative process. It is merely meant to be suggestive.

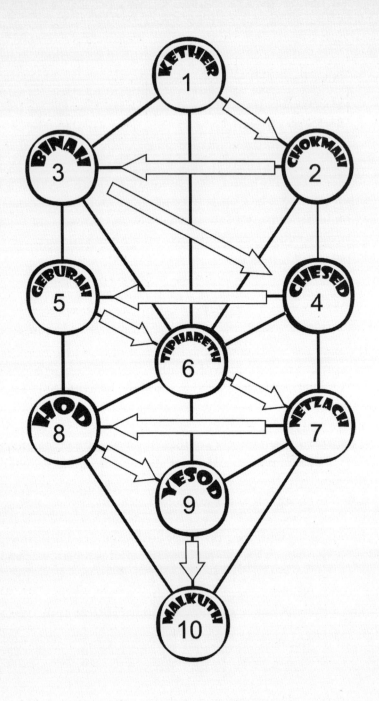

Figure 5. The Qabalistic Tree of Life.

Number	Sephiroth	Astrological Correspondence	Characteristics
1	Kether, Crown	Whole Universe	Unity
2	Chokmah, Wisdom	Zodiac	Father, expansion, free flow of creation
3	Binah, Understanding	♄ Saturn	Mother, limitation, field or womb of creation
4	Chesed, Mercy	♃ Jupiter	Beginnings of time and space
5	Geburah, Severity	♂ Mars	Beginnings of force and motion in space/time
6	Tiphareth, Beauty	☉ Sun	Son, the center, balance, beginning of individuation
7	Netzach, Victory	♀ Venus	Attraction of forces, gravity, electro magnetism, etc.
8	Hod, Splendor	☿ Mercury	Laws of the universal structure, mathematics, physics
9	Yesod, Foundation	☾ Moon	Astral or aethyric matrix
10	Malkuth, Kingdom	⊕ Earth	Daughter, the physical world

Table 5. The ten sephiroth and their correspondences.

Number	Greek God	Egyptian God	Hindu God	Nordic God
1	Zeus	Ptah	Parabrahm	Wotan
2	Uranus	Thoth	Shiva	Odin
3	Demeter	Isis	Shakti	Frigga
4	Poseidon	Amoun	Brahma	Bragi
5	Ares	Horus	Vishnu	Thor
6	Apollo	Ra	Krishna	Frey
7	Aphrodite	Hathor	Lalita	Freya
8	Hermes	Thoth	Hanuman	Loki
9	Diana	Shu	Ganesha	Frija
10	Persephone	Osiris	Lakshmi	Vidar

Table 6. The ten sephiroth and their corresponding deities.

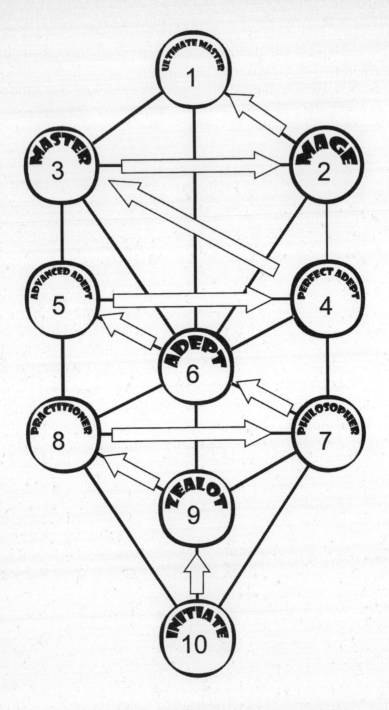

Figure 6. The process of integration and awakening shown on the Tree of Life.

In the New Hermetics, you will systematically evolve your consciousness up through the sephiroth from the tenth sephirah of physical manifestation to the first sephirah of divine unity. Each of the levels of the New Hermetics deals with one of these sephiroth and the corresponding states of consciousness and practices that allow you to understand and integrate its special nature. The process of initiation or awakening to universal consciousness is reciprocal to the process of creation. Creation begins with the unmanifest singularity of the cosmic mind, and develops into the myriad forms of physical reality. The process of the New Hermetics system will assist you in returning your consciousness from the myriad forms of the physical world back to the singularity of cosmic oneness (see figure 6, opposite).

10—Malkuth: Level 1 Initiate

This is the final sephirah in the process of creation. It is the physical universe as we know it and the sphere of the four elements. The gateway to the astral plane, or aethyr, leads off from this sephirah. It is the ultimate manifestation of the divine expression. It is also sometimes called Malkah, the Bride, or the Daughter. It is associated with the ancient element of earth, which can be understood as physical consciousness and the perceptions and images that you perceive, both externally in the world and in your mind's eye. At the Initiate level of the New Hermetics, you are instructed in the physical actions that will help to enrich you spiritually, in setting goals for your life in the world and in reframing your perceptions of pain and pleasure so that you will have greater control over your physical life and the ancient element of earth. You are instructed in how to gain balance between the ancient elements in your personality and character, in how to gain control over your inner senses, your experience of the astral plane or aethyr, and in how to visualize. All of the tools that you will use at the Initiate level give you a practical understanding of the sephirah Malkuth.

9—Yesod: Level 2 Zealot

The sephirah Yesod is the subtle framework or foundation upon which the physical universe is based. It is associated with the energies upon which the material world depends for coherence. In our bodies, these are our sensations, emotions and feelings, and the ideas that result in manifestation. For example, if your emotions do not support your ideas and dreams, they will never manifest in the world, because your ideas will not pass through the sephirah Yesod. This emotional world is the gateway between matter and spirit. Emotions are expressions of our minds and spirits, but they cause real chemical changes in our bodies that are the difference between health and disease, bliss and depression, action and hesitation. We can also change our physical bodies in ways that change our emotions, and thus change our minds and spirits. We can do this by moving in ways that energize us, activating the subtle currents of the sephiroth Yesod. At the Zealot level of the New Hermetics, you are taught how to manage and transform your emotions in numerous ways so that you are in greater control of your emotional life and of the ancient element of water. You will also begin to learn how to create magical changes through the practice called "manifesting synchronicity." Through these practices at the Zealot level, you master the sephirah Yesod.

8—Hod: Level 3 Practitioner

This sephirah comprises the laws and formulas of the universe. It is the divine intellect, the mathematical systems and concepts that form the universe as we know it. It corresponds, of course, with our own intellect, and the symbols, rules, and languages with which we all communicate and understand the world. It can be understood as the symbol systems and beliefs that we use to construct our perceptions of the world. At the Practitioner level of the New Hermetics, you are introduced to the archetypal symbology of the tarot and taught how to change your beliefs to give you greater power over your perceptions and control over your own life. You are also taught several ways to begin to use your growing powers and understanding of the universe to change your reality in a practical way and techniques for expanding and dramatically changing your mind's perceptions.

7—Netzach: Level 4 Philosopher

This sephirah is the power of attraction between the forces that shape the universe. It is the sephirah of love. It is the attractive force that binds atomic particles together, keeps planets in their orbits, and draws lovers together in passionate embrace. In our minds, the sephirah Netzach represents the passions of our hearts, the morals and values that guide our lives, our driving emotions, our intuitions, and the highest aspirations of our nature. It is also associated with the ancient element of fire, which is our will, our passion, and our creativity. At the Philosopher level of the New Hermetics, you are instructed in the process of examining and adjusting the hierarchy of your values, so that they most effectively support the kind of life you want to create. You will also learn the method for invoking the forces and presence of the ancient gods, the importance of correspondences in the creation of talismans or magical objects, and the development of your intuition. You will begin to harmonize what you have learned and begin the practice called Rising on the Planes.

6—Tiphareth: Level 5 Adept

This is the sephirah of harmony and beauty. It is the center of the Tree of Life and is associated with the Sun. It is the balancing and harmonizing power in the universe, often called compassion or bliss. Tiphareth is sometimes called The Son, because it is a reflection of the highest divine consciousness that exists in the first sephirah, Kether. This is the true center of human consciousness, and the sphere where we gain contact with the highest aspect of ourselves. It is our connection with universal consciousness, sometimes called our Holy Guardian Angel. At the Adept level of the New Hermetics, you are instructed in how to gain pure contact with this cosmic consciousness and how to resolve and master the subtle demons of fear that still hide in the dark corners of your being. From the exalted perspective of higher consciousness, your fears and personal demons will become your faithful servants. You will also further balance your nature to become truly adept and learn to radiate Rosicrucian love out into the world.

5—Geburah: Level 6 Advanced Adept

Geburah is the strength of divine consciousness—force in its most pure and undifferentiated state. It is the power of justice, the judgment of the divine. It is the will of God. In consciousness, it is the higher will of divine universal consciousness as it is expressed through the work of the Advanced Adept. The tools of the Advanced Adept are beyond the scope of this book.

4—Chesed: Level 7 Perfect Adept

This sephirah is the pure, giving, and merciful nature of divine consciousness, which gives purely of itself to create the universe. Chesed is form in its most pure and undifferentiated state, the beginnings of time and space. It is the sephirah of leadership, generosity, and abundance. The Perfect Adept is a leader in every sense of the word, dedicated to giving all to humanity. The tools of the Perfect Adept are also beyond the scope of this book.

3—Binah: Level 8 Master

This sephirah is the quantum field in which the universe manifests—the womb in which creation takes place. Binah is sometimes called The Mother. It is the beginnings of form, the start of structure in the creation of the universe. It is the last dwelling of pure divine consciousness before it expresses itself through the time-space continuum in Chesed. The Master of the New Hermetics is fully identified with this divine consciousness and identifies purely with divinity.

2—Chokmah: Level 9 Mage

This sephirah is the beginning of force. It is sometimes called The Father. It is the pure expression of divine consciousness flowing freely in the act of creation. It is not until it reaches Binah that it has any limitation. The Mage is a pure force of nature, the expression and expresser of divine creativity.

1—Kether: Level 10 Ultimate Master

This is the first sephirah, which is pure unity consciousness without differentiation. It is singularity, the monad, the universe as one thing. As it expresses itself, it moves instantly into Chokmah and Binah. Kether and the Ultimate Master are really entirely inexplicable in words, at least by me. This is really true of Binah and Chokmah as well.

TWENTY-TWO LETTERS AND PATHS

Between the spheres or sephiroth of the Tree of Life are twenty-two paths, corresponding with the twenty-two letters of the Hebrew alphabet and the twenty-two tarot trumps. These paths represent the subjective experiences that you undergo as you travel between the sephiroth in

Path	Hebrew Letter	Tarot Card	Astrological Sign	Characteristics
1	א Aleph "A"	The Fool	△ Air	Cosmic ecstasy
2	ב Beth "B"	The Magician	☿ Mercury	Cosmic knowledge
3	ג Gimel "G"	The High Priestess	☽ Moon	Divine presence
4	ד Daleth "D"	The Empress	♀ Venus	Cosmic love
5	ה Heh "H"	The Emperor	♈ Aries	Cosmic strength
6	ו Vau "V, U"	The Hierophant	♉ Taurus	Power to initiate
7	ז Zayin "Z"	The Lovers	♊ Gemini	The chymical wedding
8	ח Cheth "Ch"	The Chariot	♋ Cancer	Giving all for wisdom
9	ט Teth "T"	Strength	♌ Leo	Learning to use power
10	י Yod "I, J, Y"	The Hermit	♍ Virgo	Absorbing power
11	כ Kaph "K"	The Wheel of Fortune	♃ Jupiter	Undoing past experience
12	ל Lamed "L"	Justice	♎ Libra	Balancing forces
13	מ Mem "M"	The Hanged Man	▽ Water	Radiating love
14	נ Nun "N"	Death	♏ Scorpio	Transcendence
15	ס Samech "S"	Temperance	♐ Sagittarius	Rising on the planes
16	ע Ayin "O"	The Devil	♑ Capricorn	Talismanic work
17	פ Peh "P"	The Tower	♂ Mars	Silencing thought
18	צ Tzaddi "Tz"	The Star	♒ Aquarius	Expanding consciousness
19	ק Qoph "Q"	The Moon	♓ Pisces	Past lives, archetypes
20	ר Resh "R"	The Sun	☉ Sun	Invoking light of self
21	ש Shin "Sh"	The Last Judgment	△, ✴ Fire, Spirit	Death and rebirth
22	ת Tau "Th"	The World	▽, ♄ Earth, Saturn	Exploring the aethyr

Table 7. The twenty-two paths of the Tree of Life.

your evolutionary development toward enlightenment. They are also representative of further archetypal energies that make up our unconscious minds. Each path is attributed to a planet, a zodiacal sign, or an element. Table 7 (above) gives the basic scheme, along with a very brief description of its practical significance within the construct of the New Hermetics. The New Hermetics skills are in order from more to less advanced. You may find it valuable to look at the associated tarot cards to get a clearer picture.

This is really a brief sketch of the majority of the work of the New Hermetics. Through the tools you will learn in the second half of this book, you will experience this whole range of powers, from exploring the aethyr to transcendence. The levels of instruction take you from sephirah to sephirah, teaching you the skills and lessons of these paths along the way (see figure 7, page 47).

TETRAGRAMMATON: FOUR TAROT SUITS, FOUR WORLDS, FOUR PARTS OF THE SOUL

The formula of Tetragrammaton has many symbolical and practical functions within the science of magick. It plays only a background part in the New Hermetics, but I thought I'd give a brief sketch so that you will have as clear an understanding as possible of the Qabalistic backdrop that supports our system.

Tetragrammaton sheds some new light on the four elements that we talked about earlier. The letters of the Tetragrammaton are representations of the four elemental weapons or suits of the tarot (see figure 8, page 48).

Each of the letters of Tetragrammaton also represents a region on the Tree of Life (see figure 9, page 49).

Although it does not really play a significant role in our system, the soul may also be divided into four parts, corresponding to the Tetragrammaton:

Chia	divine spark, answering to Chokmah and yod.
Neschamah	higher aspirations of the soul, answering to Binah and heh.
Ruach	mind and reasoning powers, answering to the six sephiroth of the microcosmic man.
Nephesch	animal instincts, answering to Malkuth and heh final.

Again, this is not something we will focus on, but the formula of Tetragrammaton also represents four different worlds or planes of reality within the Qabala.

Yod is the world of Atziluth, the divine world of source.
Heh is the world of Briah, the archetypal or causal world of power.
Vau is the world of Yetzirah, the astral world of image.

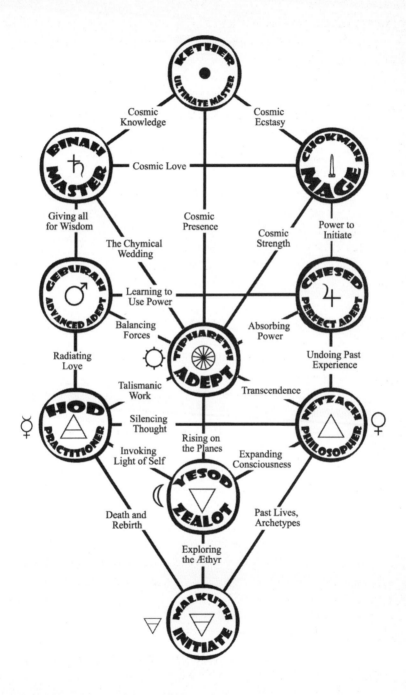

Figure 7. The levels of New Hermetic instruction on the Tree of Life.

יהוה

 י YOD is the wand of fire, the will of the magician.

ה HEH is the cup of water, the feelings of the magician.

ו VAU is the sword of air, the reason of the magician.

ה HEH is the pentacle of earth, the physical vehicle of the magician.

Earth   Air   Water   Fire

Figure 8. The Tetragrammaton, the elements, and the suits of the tarot.

Heh final is the world of Assiah, the physical world of manifestation.

Hopefully, this very brief sketch of the Qabala of the New Hermetics has begun to form a picture in your mind of the backbone of the program. Don't worry if any of this seems confusing. There will be no quiz on these subjects. I just wanted to provide a little background information for the curious. I do highly recommend that you study the Qabala more deeply than is possible in this volume. The books in the Qabala section of the bibliography are an excellent place to start.

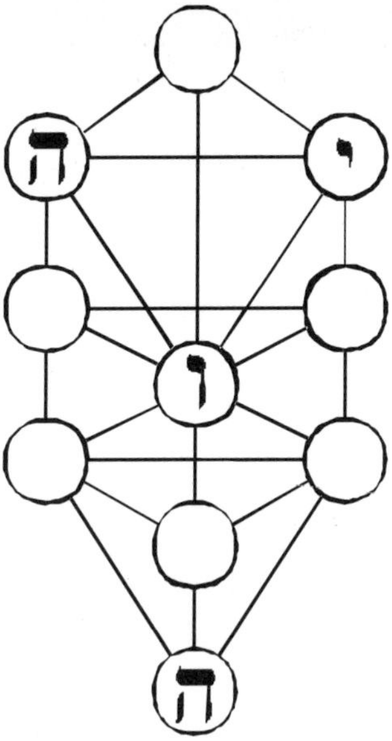

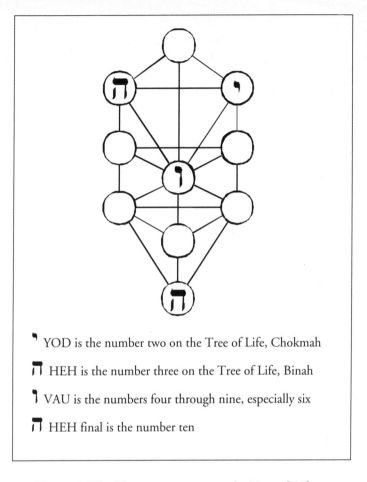

י YOD is the number two on the Tree of Life, Chokmah

ה HEH is the number three on the Tree of Life, Binah

ו VAU is the numbers four through nine, especially six

ה HEH final is the number ten

Figure 9. The Tetragrammaton on the Tree of Life.

CHAPTER 3

MODERN MODELS FOR THE NEW HERMETICS

The New Hermetics models itself on several paths to self-realization, some modern, some ancient. In this chapter, we will explore three of the primary sources for our system, neuro-linguistic programming (NLP), psychology, and modern magick.

NEURO-LINGUISTIC PROGRAMMING (NLP)

NLP is the study of the underlying structures of subjective experience and a set of tools that can be used to understand and change our experience. It was first created in the 1970s by a general semanticist named John Grinder and a computer student and informal Gestalt therapist named Richard Bandler. By modeling the communication techniques of several highly skilled psychotherapists, they created a system for understanding and changing experience that is truly astounding.

Representational Systems or Modalities

Our representational systems are our five senses. In NLP, these are usually called modalities. They are:

Seeing	Visual
Hearing	Auditory
Feeling	Kinesthetic
Smelling	Olfactory
Tasting	Gustatory

We primarily process and orient ourselves in our world through our visual, auditory, and kinesthetic senses, while our senses of smell and taste remain largely in the background of consciousness. For this reason, NLP concerns itself for the most part with the first three. However, the other two do have a powerful subconscious influence on us, so they should not be ignored. Our sense of smell particularly has a profound effect on our consciousness, and the consistent use of appropriate incense can dramatically improve our success. You may wish to choose a specific incense and use it as your own throughout the program. You can also use different incenses for specific archetypal energies. There are a few suggestions given in the Philosopher level of instruction.

Each of us uses certain of the three main senses more than others. Some people are more visual, while others are more kinesthetic, or "feeling-oriented." By understanding which representational systems or modalities we use the most, we can understand more clearly how to help ourselves learn, grow, and change most effectively.

The NLP visual, auditory, and kinesthetic modalities correspond rather well with the alchemical principles of sulphur, mercury, and salt. When we are processing our consciousness with our visual sense or modality (looking at things or making pictures in our minds), we tend to be operating with the principle of sulphur. We process quickly and vigorously, deleting superfluous information from our awareness, and are highly energetic. When we are processing our consciousness with our auditory sense or modality (hearing things or talking internally to ourselves), we tend to be operating with the principle of mercury. We process fluidly, evaluating what we are experiencing and carefully integrating it into our understanding. When we are processing our consciousness with our kinesthetic sense or modality (feeling things physically or emotionally), we tend to be operating with the principle of salt. We process slowly and carefully, we feel heavy, slow, and sometimes even "stuck." But this is all only meant to be suggestive.

It is very easy to get an idea of your dominant modality, although it does change in different circumstances of your life. However, if you ask yourself what you like most about your house or your mate or your job, you can begin to get an idea. If you answer that you like the way he looks or the beautiful architecture or a sense of adventure, you are probably operating primarily in the visual modality. If you say you like the fact that your house is in a quiet place or that you like the nice things your girlfriend says to you or that you get to talk on the phone all day, then you are probably operating in auditory mode. If you say your job makes you feel good and you love the way your boyfriend hugs you or that your house just has a positive "vibe," then you are probably operating out of your kinesthetic sense. But we all do use all of our senses, so please don't go away thinking that you're a "visual" person and start trying to ignore the rest of your senses. We all use all five senses, but some of these senses are simply stronger and tend to drive us more in our daily lives.

Another way of discovering our use of the different modalities is through eye-accessing cues. Bandler and Grinder discovered that, when we are using different modalities, we tend to move our eyes in certain directions. Our eyes seem to direct the flow of our consciousness and will move as we change the modalities we are using to focus on the world:

Vr: visual remembered, when we are seeing an image that we remember in our minds we tend to look up and to the left.
Vc: visual constructed, when we are constructing an image (or visualizing, clairvoyance), we tend to look up and to the right.
Ar: auditory remembered, when we are remembering some sound that we have heard, we tend to look to our left.
Ac: auditory constructed, when we are mentally constructing some new sound (or using clairaudience), we tend to look to the right.
Ad: auditory digital, when we are speaking to ourselves (internal dialogue), we tend to look down to the right.
K: kinesthetic, when we are feeling something, emotions or physical sensations, we tend to look down to the left.

Figure 10 (see page 54) illustrates the point.

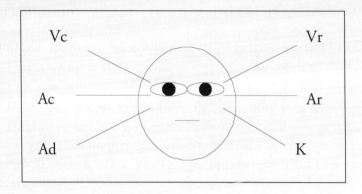

Figure 10. The eye-accessing cues for NLP modalities.

This is only an approximation of experience. Some people are wired differently and will use different eye-accessing cues. For instance, many left-handed people are simply wired oppositely. If you are ever having trouble performing visualization techniques, try setting your eyes in appropriate directions to help you access your abilities most fully. This is an excellent aid to the New Hermeticist. It should be added that, when we are recalling or mentally creating a smell, we tend to focus our eyes on our noses, and when we are recalling or mentally creating a taste, we tend to focus on our tongues or palettes.

Submodalities

Each of the senses or modalities has variations, distinctions, and qualitative differences. These are called submodalities in NLP. They are the fine details of how we process the world. In other words, if you close your eyes right now and visualize a kitten, there are nearly infinite ways that you can see it. It may be dim or bright, in color or black and white, close to you or far away. It may be in a frame or in a panoramic view. These are the submodalities of your visualization. Here is a selection of submodalities for the three main modalities:

Visual: moving or still, panoramic or framed, size, brightness, distance, intensity of color, color or black-and-white, contrast, angle, focus, self in or out of picture

Auditory: volume, rhythm, inflection, tempo, tonality, location, timbre, consistency
Kinesthetic: temperature, texture, vibration, pressure, duration, intensity, weight, location

These are some of the ways that we can experience something. What's more, if you are experiencing something in a way that is unsatisfying, you can change the submodality of that experience and entirely change your understanding of it. Using your natural and simple ability to change these submodalities greatly increases your own effectiveness when using New Hermetics technologies. If you are visualizing a blue ball of Jupiterean energy and it seems dim, far away, or weak, you can simply turn up these submodalities and experience the energy more powerfully. This will transform and empower your mind in ways that you can't even imagine yet.

States

The ability to change our states of consciousness is fundamental to the New Hermetics. The technologies that you will soon explore are simply many different states of consciousness. The New Hermetics is essentially based on the fact that all mystical phenomena are states of consciousness and that, by moving our minds into these states, we obtain the rewards of mysticism and magick. In our lives, we usually travel from one state of consciousness to another without any real control or even an awareness that we are changing. Happiness, excitement, enthusiasm, motivation, inner peace, and illumination are all just states. We all have characteristic strategies for getting into these states. We also have strategies for getting into unresourceful states such as boredom, depression, sadness, and stress.

These states literally run our lives. Without learning to manage them effectively, our lives are emotional roller coasters that travel between peaks of joy and valleys of despair. With the New Hermetics, you will learn to access states that you never realized were available to you, and you will be able to rid yourself of patterns of negative states. Learning to access powerful states and eliminate negative ones is literally the most important thing you can ever do in your life.

Essentially, there are two ways to change your state. The first is to change your physiology. By changing your posture, the way you move, and the way that you breathe, you can rapidly change your state. If you want to become depressed, breathe shallowly, droop your head and shoulders, and move slowly and lethargically. If you want to be in an excited state, get up, stretch, open your chest, breathe deeply, and wave your arms around enthusiastically. It can be that easy. To get into a meditative state, sit down, straighten your spine, relax your body, and close your eyes, focusing inward. You immediately start changing your state.

The second way to change your state is through your mental focus. If you think about all the bad things that have happened in your life or all the starving babies in the world, your can enter into a negative state. If you think of all the people who love you, all the nice things you've ever done, and how much your life is going to change for the positive with the New Hermetics, you can get into a very resourceful state. These two ways illustrate the fact that our emotions are literally the gateway between mind and matter. By changing our material conditions, we can change our minds, or vice versa.

Reframing

We understand the world around us by placing it within a frame of reference. These frames provide us with the context for understanding our experience. For the most part, when something challenging or sad happens, people frame that experience as bad or negative. However, it must be understood that this frame is a choice. People choose to frame things as bad or good with their own minds and choices. It is also possible to frame any challenging experience as educational or evolutionary, because we always have the opportunity to change for the positive with any experience.

In NLP, the process of creating more empowering frames for our experience is called reframing, and many of the New Hermetics technologies are based on reframing our experiences so that they empower rather than debilitate us. We can reframe our past experiences so that they give us greater strength for the future. We can reframe our current experiences so that they provide us with new opportunities. We can reframe our future experiences so that we do not repeat our mistakes.

Reframing gives us the power to shape our lives in the image that we want.

It is possible to reframe your experiences by changing their sub-modalities, as mentioned before. It is also possible to reframe our experiences by changing their context. If you get fired from your job, you can see it as a tragedy that threatens your life. However, you can also see it as an opportunity to have new experiences and perhaps a better job. You can also frame it that your employers have made a monumental mistake and feel very sorry for them. By changing the frame, you change the way you feel about a situation. This provides you with greater choice and freedom and gives you access to more resourceful states.

Anchors

Anchors are parts of an experience that have the ability to bring back the full state associated with that experience. When you hear a song that "brings you back" to a special time in your life, this is an anchor. When you smell something that triggers a forgotten memory, this is an anchor. When you are in the presence of your mother for five seconds and you are already annoyed, this is an anchor. When someone touches you in a special way that instantly makes you feel loved, this is an anchor. We all have hundreds and hundreds of anchors that shift our consciousness into both resourceful and unresourceful states.

NLP uses the concept of anchors to help people access resourceful states automatically. Basically, if you are in any extreme state of emotion, any unique stimulus at that time will create an anchor. For instance, if you are feeling really ecstatic, totally in a state of bliss, and I squeeze your hand and say, "lima bean," you will then associate this hand-squeezing and the words "lima bean" with this ecstatic state. If I want to send you back to that ecstatic state later, I merely squeeze your hand and say "lima bean," in the exact same way I did it before, and you will automatically re-access that state.

Advertisers use the concept of anchoring all the time. They attempt to associate their product with all sorts of things from sex to pleasure to rock and roll. In the New Hermetics, you learn to anchor and automatically access a number of positive states, including meditation, creativity, peace of mind, vitality, and communication.

To create an anchor, just follow these simple guidelines:

1. Make sure the state or experience is intense and pure.
2. Create a unique stimulus.
3. Anchor at the peak of the state or experience.
4. Use exactly the same stimulus when you want to access
    the state in the future.

There are many other aspects of NLP that have also been incorporated into the New Hermetics, such as techniques for establishing rapport, pacing and leading, meta-programs, timelines, the NLP presuppositions, and others. These have been imbedded into the structure of the New Hermetics training and are really only necessary to understand in later phases of your work.

PSYCHOLOGICAL METAPHORS: JUNG, REICH, AND LEARY

The three primary psychological metaphors that lie at the base of the New Hermetics are found in the systems of Carl Jung, Wilhelm Reich, and Timothy Leary. Each has contributed in a unique way to the theory and practice of self-realization.

Jung and the Collective Unconscious

Psychologist Carl Jung first promulgated the idea of the "collective unconscious" in the first half of the 20th century. The basic concept is that, at a deep level of mind, all humans share the same basic reality structure. This shared mind is the collective unconscious. It is from this collective mind that the "archetypes" spring. In ancient times, these archetypes took the form of gods and goddesses that demanded respect and worship. These archetypal figures still exist in our deep minds and form the basis of our unconscious drives and desires.

Each of us experiences these archetypes in dreams and in voices, images, or feelings that come into our minds. The archetypes populate and dominate our inner worlds. Each of us has an archetypal lover, an archetypal father and mother, etc. In many of us, these archetypes are repressed or obsess us in unhealthy ways. In the New Hermetics you will become more and more in touch with the collective unconscious, and you will have the opportunity to heal your relationships with these extremely powerful forces in your life. As you become more aware of them, you will understand your own psyche and the psyches of those around you. This will increase your power in the inner and the outer world immensely.

We often project these archetypes onto people in our lives, people such as bosses, lovers, parents, and friends. This creates much of the tension and difficulty that we experience in life. By understanding and working with the archetypes of the collective unconscious directly, you can learn to experience the outer world without your projections and be able to balance and heal your inner world.

Wilhelm Reich, the Orgone, and Character Armor

Wilhelm Reich's theory of the orgone and human body armor is very important to the New Hermetics. In the 1930s, Reich discovered what he considered the "life energy" in an extensive series of experiments. He called it "orgone." He believed that this orgone flows abundantly through the body of a mentally healthy human being. However, most of us hold tension and stress in areas of our body. Reich called this "character armor." This habitual tension causes the flow of orgone to be impaired, resulting in numerous health problems, from neuroses to cancer.

Reich's orgone theory is very similar to the ancient theories of life energy. The ancients called this life energy *prana, chi, pneuma, ruach* or *spiritus* in different cultures. All of these words translate approximately to "breath."

In the New Hermetics, you will learn several techniques of breathing and freeing yourself of energy blocks. This will enhance your mental and physical health immeasurably, as well as free you from "armor" and stress. Movement is also important for releasing habitual tensions, and a number of techniques will direct you to move in novel ways that will stimulate change.

Timothy Leary and the Eight-circuit Model of Consciousness

Timothy Leary's eight-circuit model of consciousness is very useful in gaining further insight into the human mind. Leary created this model of consciousness based on the idea that we humans have eight separate mini-brains or circuits that handle various functions in our consciousness. It is merely a model and is not meant to imply that we actually

Bio-circuit	Evolutionary Process	Activation in Human Growth	Area of Consciousness	Driving Forces
I **Biosurvival**	one-celled life	infant	sucking, nourishment, cuddling	pain/pleasure
II **Emotional-territorial**	vertebrate life	toddler	power struggles	dominance/submission
III **Semantic**	early primate, language and tools	child	learning, calculation	intelligence/stupidity
IV **Socio-sexual**	urbanized civilization	post-pubescent domesticity	morality, reproduction, pair-bonding	right/wrong
V **Neurosomatic**	neurological and somatic consciousness explorers	ecstatic consciousness	bliss, somatic rapture	euphoria
VI **Neuroelectric**	advanced consciousness engineers	meta-programming consciousness	reprogramming self, relativization of reality	creativity
VII **Neurogenetic**	superior consciousness engineers	evolutionary consciousness	collective unconscious	evolution
VIII **Neuroatomic**	superlative consciousness engineers	quantum consciousness	non-local awareness, cosmic union	omnipresence

Table 8. Leary's eight-circuit model of consciousness.

have multiple brains, but rather that the functions of our brains can be conveniently compartmentalized into eight distinct units.

Each circuit is based on a period in the evolution of consciousness from the simple state of the amoeba to the infinitely complex spiritual minds of human beings. Leary felt that each of us goes through the whole process of evolution from amoeboid consciousness to fully human consciousness (circuits 1-4) as we grow from infancy to adulthood. But this evolution involves only the first four circuits. There are four more circuits that allow for our further evolution into fully self-actualized cosmic beings. Table 8 (above) shows the eight circuits, the evolutionary process, the stages in human growth, the areas of consciousness, and driving forces with which each circuit is concerned.

Bio-circuit	Qabalistic Sephira	New Hermetics Level	Power
I Biosurvival	10. Malkuth	Initiate	control of pain and pleasure
II Emotional-territorial	9. Yesod	Zealot	control of emotions
III Semantic	8. Hod	Practitioner	control of beliefs
IV Socio-sexual	7. Netzach	Philosopher	control of values
V Neurosomatic	6. Tiphareth	Adept	communion with cosmic consciousness
VI Neuroelectric	5. Geburah	Advanced Adept	creativity within cosmic consciousness
VII Neurogenetic	4. Chesed	Perfect Adept	integration within cosmic consciousness
VIII Neuroatomic	3. Binah	Master	identification with cosmic consciousness

Table 9. Leary's eight-circuit model and the New Hermetics.

Most of us are only consciously aware of the first four circuits, while the more advanced circuits lay dormant forming our unconscious minds until we are awakened to their use.

These eight circuits also correspond to the lower eight sephiroth on the Qabalistic Tree of Life. In the New Hermetics, you will be brought progressively into complete awareness and control of all of your eight circuits. In the first four levels of the New Hermetics, you will be taught how to reframe and recondition the functions of these first four circuits, and in the later levels, you will learn how to experience and utilize the higher circuits. Table 9 (above) summarizes the relationships between the two systems.

MAGICK: PSYCHOLOGY AND SPIRITUALITY

There has been some confusion about whether the New Hermetics is a psychological or a spiritual system. It is really just an issue of models. In the psychological model, magick is viewed as entirely being "in our heads," while in the spiritual model, it is viewed as a connection with an admittedly invisible but very real and tangible spiritual world.

Many modern occultists view magick in more or less psychological terms, seeing it as a sort of colorful mental philosophy. The New Hermetics agrees with this wholeheartedly, but we do not wish to discard the spiritual model either. There are many phenomena that occur that defy our current scientific understanding of the universe. You may perform acts of magick, and you will get unexpectedly positive results. I can personally guarantee that you will continually be surprised. Still, many of the good skeptics among you may view these occurrences as coincidence.

However, if you pretend to have magical powers, and your current belief system prefers the psychological model, you will frequently experience inexplicable synchronicities that indicate that there may be something more going on beyond it being "all in your head." But if you approach these experiments believing completely in the awesome powers of magick, you may find that you fail often enough that it is impossible to prove your powers statistically.

We reconcile this in the New Hermetics by pointing out that there is really no fundamental difference between the models. As a great occultist once said, "It's all in your head, you just don't realize how big your head really is." The spiritual world is in our minds, but so is the physical world. By changing conditions in the internal, spiritual world, you eventually create change in the physical world.

To demonstrate, spend the next ten to fifteen minutes focused on how nice the people who live in your neighborhood are. If you really focus on this intently, you may discover something remarkable. If you spend some time really thinking about all of the times when people have been kind to you and all of the pleasant experiences you have had with both friends and strangers, and that you have even had experiences where you did not get along with someone initially, but eventually you were good friends, you may feel pretty positive. And if you really focus, so that your feelings, images, and memories are vivid and powerful, you may feel very positive. Then go outside. You may find an amazing transformation. You may see friends and potential friends everywhere you look. With this simple mental process, you can transform your entire neighborhood! Now, we do this with ourselves and the negative opposite of this all the time. What you focus on transforms your reality. Just by being aware of this, you can become all-powerful whenever you are ready.

It can be argued that you are not really changing the world by this process, just your own mind, but this is really irrelevant. The moment that you have a pleasant experience with a stranger after you have done this exercise, you experience what Jung called a "synchronicity." You have created an intentional, meaningful coincidence. This is the essence of magick. And argue as you may about cause and effect, you have made the change happen. By projecting positive thoughts into the universe, you cause positive experiences in your life. It is really quite simple and works with all things.

Words, Colors, and Brain Change

The New Hermetics offers many more sophisticated methods of manifesting synchronicity (or magick) than the above creative visualization. It should be emphasized that simple creative visualization is an incredibly potent and surprisingly effective technique. Still, with the New Hermetics, you will be introduced to several methods of more distinctly connecting with particular kinds of archetypal energy to manifest specific kinds of synchronicities.

One of the most powerful ways of specifying your magical or mystical intent is through the use of words. We humans are verbal creatures. By instructing our unconscious minds with specific desires, worded carefully, we can manifest exactly what we want. Words can be used in many ways. They can be used rhythmically to create chants, incantations, invocations, or mantras. They can be used to describe, and thus summon, the energy of some specific god. Words can be combined to create glyphs representing our desires in abstract, pictorial form. You can create magical words by understanding the archetypal, Qabalistic energies of each letter.

However, one of the most simple and effective uses of words is to literally describe our experience or the experience that we would like to have. If you describe an experience vividly, you experience it, because in order to reference the memory, you must return to the experience. In other words, if I ask you to describe an experience of deep relaxation in complete detail, down to every nuance of feeling, you have to experience it in order to describe it. As you describe each nuance, you are relaxing more and more, just to access greater detail. By creating simple instructions that guide us to experiences that we desire, we can literally transform our lives from within. We can even use this specialized language to create invocations, mantras, or other spiritually minded word constructions that are automatically transformational. This is exactly what the New Hermetics has done with the tools you will study in the rest of this book. Constructing experience with language is built into the fabric of our consciousness, and if you consciously take control of this, there is no limit to what you can do.

The power of color is also strong in effecting change in our brains and in our lives. It has been proved in studies that, when office walls are painted blue, employees complain that the temperature is too cold. If the walls are then painted yellow or red, employees start complaining that it is too hot, even though the temperature is exactly the same in both cases! In fact, many colors used in signs, traffic signals, and other practical institutions of government and business have been carefully researched to create maximum effect in human response. There is a definite correlation between certain colors and certain emotional states and even physiological functions.

> **Red:** Aggressiveness, conquest, force, vigor, energy, warmth, love; stimulates, excites, and warms the body, increases heart rate, blood pressure, brain activity, and respiration.
> **Orange:** Success, expanding interests and activities; stimulates the appetite and reduces fatigue, lifts energy level.
> **Yellow:** Creativity, self-confidence and courage, inspiration; stimulates memory, raises blood pressure and pulse rate, cheers you up.
> **Green:** Vibrant color of life and growth; has universal appeal to our sense of balance and normality, soothing and relaxing body/mind, helps the aging to feel more vibrant.
> **Blue:** Creative force, peace, maturity, calmness, dependability, color of pineal gland, color of spirit, calming effect on body; lowers

blood pressure, heart rate, and respiration, has a profound cooling effect.

Violet: Spiritual color; soothes organs, relaxes muscles, and calms the nervous system.

People have used color to create magick and to inspire religious feeling since the earliest times. In the New Hermetics, you will use specific colors for creating specific effects based on modern research as well as ancient Hermetic and Qabalistic correspondences. They correspond almost exactly. We all naturally associate color with universal archetypal energies. The tendency is built right into our brains. We involuntarily associate red with energy, passion, expression, blood. We associate blue with tranquility, the sky, water, peace. We associate green with jealousy and, by analogy, desire—also growth, nature, and, with Americans, even money. I could go on and on, but I'm sure you've picked up what I mean. The power of color is so pervasive and effective that it is sometimes all that is necessary to cause changes in yourself and your world.

Mind Travel, Aethyr, or the Astral Plane

The real secret of magick is that it is much simpler than most people could ever believe possible. This automatically protects its mysteries from the foolish who chase after complex "occult" theories or who dismiss it, calling it "mere imagination."

In fact, the whole of magick is summed up quite well in those two words, "mere imagination." Magick is the science of imagination. In order to develop magical powers, it is only necessary to develop your imagination into a finely tuned instrument, and then to direct your will through your imaginings. I know, it sounds too simple, but really, this is what it is. There are some who may argue with me on this, but I can assure you that they are most definitely not really practicing magick.

You see, the aethyr that I have mentioned a few times is really just your imagination, the world that you enter when you close your eyes. There is a bit more to it. The part of your imagination with which you are familiar is only the beginning of your true inner world. After you work with the New Hermetics for a time, you will discover deeper and deeper layers of your imagination. You will encounter other worlds and archetypal figures, beings of light and of darkness. Some of these beings and landscapes will seem to be just figments, but others will have a uniquely compelling quality. These deeper, more compelling visions will be such powerful experiences that you will be transformed by merely encountering them.

However, even the fleeting images of your undeveloped imagination are sources of incredible power. All of the forces in your mind are transformative. You should consider every internal experience in your mind and body as a successful act of magick. Then you will begin to understand your immense power and responsibility. If you create images, words, and feelings of power, you will be powerful. If you create images, words, and feelings of depression, you will be depressed. Our brains are so incredibly effective at creating the realities that we imagine for ourselves that most of us don't even realize our responsibility. If you learn to direct your thoughts in new and empowering directions, your life will transform. I guarantee it.

When you are using the New Hermetics' tools, even if you only seem to be pretending when you see an image of the goddess Venus, please realize that this pretend image is still powerful for transforming your life. If you allow yourself to experience the most vivid imaginary experience of the Goddess of Love that you can create, you will be experiencing the Goddess of Love.

If you are practicing astral projection, you may feel that you are just pretending to leave your body. This is perfectly okay. You may still feel yourself sitting in your chair as you imagine your astral body floating upward. Just stay with your imagination and you will succeed in your magick. Do not worry about "silver cords" or any of the other fanciful descriptions of many occult writers. I have experimented with astral projection for over fifteen years, and I have experienced "complete separation" many times. But I have also had totally successful astral journeys that started with me "just pretending" to leave my body. I've discovered that there really isn't any difference once you get involved in a vision. Just imagining that you are in your astral body will soon result in a realization that you have left your body far behind.

Emotional Energy

Most of us are really rather tormented beings. We have conflicting impulses, morals, values, and beliefs. We struggle with self-doubt, sadness, anger, boredom, and all sorts of other mental conflicts. Basically, all of these struggles are based on fear. We fear rejection, loneliness, death, physical threats, and a million other things. All of these fears lodge themselves in our bodies and block our awareness completely from the love and bliss that are waiting there for us to discover.

Synchronistically, the places where we experience our fears in our bodies correspond roughly to the seven Eastern chakras. We feel the loss of a loved one in our hearts, physical threats in our stomachs, intellectual fears in our foreheads, etc.

These unpleasant bodily sensations are really natural helpers that are there to assist us—to warn us of impending danger, to tell us that we are involved in unhealthy situations. However, because of the complexity of our human brains, we apply these same fear signals to entirely internally created and unreal threats. We have become so habitually fearful that we misfire these warning pains all the time. We experience fear and anxiety when it is unnecessary and not useful to us. We have unintentionally instructed a part of ourselves to give us a pain signal in some situation, and this part continues to fire off this signal, this old instruction, in situations where it is totally unnecessary and no longer useful. How many of us have felt frightened at the thought of approaching an attractive member of the opposite sex? That attractive person is most likely not going to harm us in any way, but we fire off the same signal we might fire off in the presence of a wild animal. This is a total misfire of a fear signal that can cripple us from getting the most out of life.

By learning to become more aware of our bodies and our emotions, we can clear ourselves of these misfires and unconstructive negative emotions. We can reframe our internal representations so that they are empowering rather than debilitating. Once we have learned how to manage our emotional states, we can really begin to experience the joys of life and become more aware of our inner power and cosmic scope. We can experience the joy of an unconflicted flow of bliss throughout our being.

CHAPTER 4
THE NEW HERMETICS PROGRAM

Now that you have been introduced to some of the key concepts of the New Hermetics, you can begin to explore the levels of training. Each of these levels focuses on the inner development of one of the sephirah of the Tree of Life, the paths that travel between them, and the corresponding bio-circuit of Leary's eight-circuit model.

In the following pages, you will also be introduced to the core tools of the New Hermetics that comprise all levels of instruction. I will refer back to these tools often in Part II of the book. These tools are specific designs for moving your consciousness through the experiences that will lead you to transcendental knowledge and power. These tools are progressive. Each intentionally follows the last. If you simply go through the tools that seem to amuse you at the moment, you will not experience the full benefits of the program. These tools are a comprehensive plan for awakening you to your inner genius and illumination. They are intended for conscientious use, not mere light reading. If you would like to read ahead or use one of the more advanced tools before doing this preliminary work, that is fine. However, your results will match your effort.

It must also be noted that these are simply tools. They are forms, like martial arts kata, for a mental karate or kung fu. In order to work properly, they must be animated by your spirit and creativity. Otherwise they are just empty. At any time, you may feel free to add anything you like to these forms, as long as you understand the core principles. It is your inner world, and you will quickly discover many significant additions to your own personal practice. You may also discover that you are already using many of these tools or something similar. The New Hermetics provides a framework in which to get the maximum evolutionary benefit from them.

THE NEW HERMETICS LEVELS OF INSTRUCTION

After mastering the core practices of the New Hermetics, you will move through the levels of instruction toward self-realization. In Part II of the book, you will find detailed practices for the first 5 levels, and a summary of the practices for the levels beyond.

Initiate Level
10—Malkuth
The First Bio-circuit

The focus in this level is your development in life, the actions necessary to develop your inner power, reframing the pain/pleasure principle, and the balancing of the four elements in your personality so that you have the greatest power of choice over your actions. You are introduced to the aethyr through visualization, astral projection, and communication with your inner teacher or inner sage. These tools are for getting the mind used to looking inward. They teach you to enter an altered state of consciousness and show you how to work in that state. These tools help you to refine your skills for visualizing and experiencing your internal world. They do not demand much of you other than doing them. They also help you to organize your inner world into a functional inner temple for changing reality. While these tools are basic, even experienced meditators and metaphysicians find tremendous value in strengthening their abilities in these areas. There is tremendous power in these elementary tools.

Zealot Level
9—Yesod
The Second Bio-circuit

This level is about understanding and managing your emotional states. It is called the Zealot level because it requires a certain amount of zeal to get through it. You are first introduced to your emotional world by confronting your greatest fear: the fear of death. Then, through breath work, movement, and refocusing the mind, you are trained to become more deeply aware of your emotional body and how to reframe your emotions into empowering, transformational tools. Powerful breathing techniques are presented that calm and balance your emotions. The New Hermetics' tool for manifesting synchronicity is also explained for your use.

Practitioner Level
8—Hod
The Third Bio-circuit

In this level, you begin to actively explore archetypes through the symbolism of the tarot. This really assists in understanding the unconscious imagery that comes up in the mind and increases your understanding of the spiritual construction of the universe. You begin to explore the nature of thought processes, beliefs, and mental symbol structures. You learn to explore past lives and to integrate the larger patterns of existence into your life. You learn how to consciously and unconsciously change your beliefs about yourself and reality and actually begin to transform your life into a powerful force. You learn to project thought forms, elemental energies, and desires outward effectively. You practice expanding your consciousness to fill the universe and silencing your mind of all thought.

Philosopher Level
7—Netzach
The Fourth Bio-circuit

At this level, you discover how the driving forces of your will are the hierarchies of values that control your morality, desires, ethics, and even your creativity. You learn to harmonize your values with your actual desires and begin to harmonize your goals, emotional states, beliefs, and values into a fully functional and non-conflicted self. You learn to create talismans, physical representations of magical synchronicities that you project out into the world. You actively invoke the powers of the ancient archetypal god-forms to balance and transform your abilities and your life. You begin to work practically with your intuition and begin the practice called Rising on the Planes.

Adept Level
6—Tiphareth
The Fifth Bio-circuit

At the Adept level, you learn to communicate consciously with cosmic consciousness, intimately and personally. You discover the infinite genius and bliss that is within us all. This has been called enlightenment, *samadhi*, illumination, Zen, the Knowledge and Conversation of Your Holy Guardian Angel, and many other names. Transformed by this experience, you fearlessly confront the remaining demons within you, transforming these fearful beasts into servants. Once and for all, you establish yourself in the light of your own genius and personal inspiration, projecting love and harmony out into the world. You also learn the all-important lesson of balancing humility and pride in your light.

Beyond Adepthood
Levels Six through Ten

The tools beyond the Adept level are not covered in this manual, but we will be happy to make them available to any adepts who have gone through the entire training program and have proved themselves to be balanced individuals who are really using the New Hermetics to transform their lives. These tools are not secret by any means and will be described in detail in a future volume. They are, however, in many cases, quite complex and involve specific technologies for working with different kinds of magick, as well as the subtle technologies for training future adepts. There are also a number of tools like Burning off your Karma and Giving up Everything for Nothing that are advanced mystical tools and natural progressions toward Mastery.

The tools in the next few chapters give you an excellent starting place in your practices and help you to truly awaken the hidden powers within you. If you conscientiously and thoroughly follow these simple instructions, you will find yourself awakening into a whole new world of spiritual power. As you read through these practical exercises, please note that I have provided simple diagrams wherever possible to illuminate the text.

THE ALTERED STATE

Nearly all of the tools of the New Hermetics are practiced in an altered state of consciousness. This is a state of deep relaxation combined with focused concentration. This state has been called the hypnagogic state, meditation, self-hypnosis, the magical trance, and many other names. It is a natural state that we all enter into quite regularly when we focus in a pleasant manner on anything. We often slip into trance when driving, exercising, reading, or doing any other activity in which we limit our attention. Regular practice of the following exercise will help you to be more relaxed in life, reduce tension, and give you an abundance of energy and tranquility. This practice forms the foundation for many of the practices you will find in Part II.

1. Sit or lie down in a quiet place where you will not be disturbed for about 20 minutes.
2. Take a few deep breaths and allow yourself to get into a comfortable position.
3. Close your eyes and take a few more long, slow deep breaths, totally settling into the position you have taken.
4. Notice the sensations in your body, and adjust your position as necessary to be completely comfortable.
5. Starting with your feet, progressively relax your entire body up to the crown of your head by feeling and visualizing a slow calming wave of energy moving soothingly up your body. You may mentally say to yourself, "My toes are relaxing, my feet are relaxing, my ankles are relaxing, etc."
6. When you have reached the crown of your head, you will be thoroughly relaxed. Feel the sensations of your body and relax any parts that have become tense again.

7. Mentally say to yourself that you are about to count down from 20 to 1, and that, when you reach 1, you will be in a deep state of relaxation and focus.
8. Slowly begin counting backward from 20, mentally saying "20, and deeper, and deeper, I am relaxing deeper, and 19, so much deeper, and 18, and deeper, and deeper, etc.," until you reach 1. Allow yourself to relax more and more deeply as you count. When you reach 1, you will be deeply in the altered state.
9. You may now enjoy this state, or go even deeper, or practice one of the upcoming tools.
10. When you are ready to return to normal awareness, simply count upward from 1 to 5, telling yourself that you will awaken refreshed and relaxed.

There are a number of other more elegant ways to achieve the altered state that you may learn with the New Hermetics, but this is the simplest and most straightforward method and a good way to start out. When you are in the altered state you may notice a number of sensations:

- Tingling, warmth, or coolness;
- A sense of lightness or heaviness;
- A lack of desire to move;
- Minor twitches in your fingers or toes;
- A feeling of slipping or floating;
- A change in breathing pattern.

These are definitive indicators of a change in your state. You may also experience other sensations. If you relax too deeply, you may experience a short period that you do not recall, but do not worry, you will return to full awareness as soon as you need to. You do not need to move to this deep a level at all to use the tools of the New Hermetics. The perfect state is one in which you are totally involved in your inner world because you are thoroughly relaxed, but not so relaxed that you drift too far into reverie. After you have practiced this exercise a few times, you will find it quite easy to do.

INITIATION

This is a very basic tool for New Hermetics self-initiation. Initiation is usually the passing of spiritual awakening, knowledge, and power from teacher directly to student, rather than something that you do on your own. Unfortunately, that is not possible within the context of a book. However, you will be able to get wonderful results from this exercise if you practice it slowly a few times and just let yourself enjoy it.

This simple tool is based upon the formula of initiation from all religions and secret societies. The candidate for initiation is in darkness and introduced slowly to the light. This is usually performed in a ceremonial manner, but in this New Hermetics self-initiation, only the internal pattern that your mind goes through in the process of initiation will be explored. However, initiation ceremonies can be very transformative on a psycho-social level as well as on an interior spiritual level, and you may find seeking out a group to be a useful pursuit.

This initiatory tool is a pure representation of the inner, spiritual initiation that takes place as a result of any ceremony performed. It allows you to dispense with any outer ceremony at all for the moment, while maintaining the true inner light of the initiatory pattern. It also enables you to eliminate any dogmatic or religious overtones from the initiatory experience, allowing you to experience initiation in whatever way is most appropriate for your needs. This specific tool is based on the desire of the candidate to experience transcendence, the purification of the candidate, and final admission into the experience of the light.

1. Enter the altered state (see above).
2. When you are in a relaxed and concentrated state, begin to visualize that you are inside a large black egg that is one or two feet taller than you. This egg represents your spiritual body or "aura." Visualize yourself surrounded by an abyss of pure darkness, floating in a void. You can, if you wish, hear the sound of waves far down below you, as if you are floating above a black sea.
3. Look up in your inner space, and begin to visualize a point of brilliant white light above you, shining down on your auric egg. This point of light represents the descent of cosmic

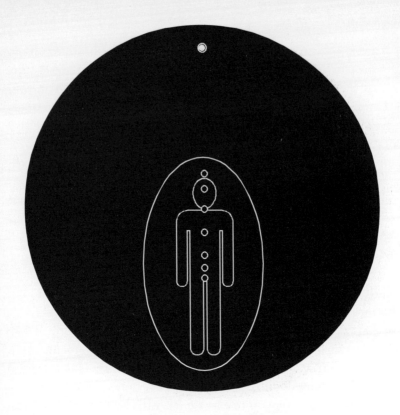

Figure 11. A point of white light represents cosmic consciousness.

consciousness. But you are still in the blackness of your own
consciousness (see figure 11, above).

4. Become aware of your desire to experience this cosmic con-
    sciousness, feeling a pleasant sensation around the area of
    your genitals and the base of your spine.

5. Begin to move this feeling of desire slowly up through your
    body, feeling the pleasant sensation moving up your back,
    through your sex organs, up into your belly. At the same
    time, visualize that the point of light above you is growing
    larger, into a globe, and moving slowly down toward you
    (see figure 12, opposite).

6. Continue feeling your desire for this light, moving it up into
    your chest and neck.

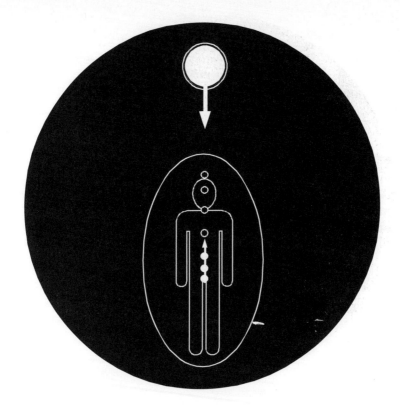

Figure 12. Feel desire for the growing light.

7. Visualize the globe of light getting larger, continuing to move slowly down toward the top of your head. As it gets closer, visualize a beam or ray of light shining down into your black auric egg, down onto the top of your head, turning your auric egg gray from this influx of light. Feel the soft light around you purifying you within and without (see figure 13, page 78).

8. Feel your desire to be with this globe of light moving up into your face and your forehead. Feel your desire all through your body mingling with the feelings of purity from the light, and transforming into euphoric bliss.

9. See and feel the globe of light entering your egg, and reaching your head. Feel an almost electric ripple at the point of

Figure 13. A ray of light shines down into your auric egg.

contact. Visualize and feel brilliant white light filling your
whole body and your auric egg (see figure 14, opposite).
10. Feel yourself enveloped in light. Yield to this light, letting it
flow pleasurably through you, and letting yourself flow into
the light. Feel yourself dissolving blissfully into light. In this
state, you may begin to receive impressions about your life's
purpose or who you really are, or you may simply feel
relaxed and euphoric (see figure 15, opposite).
11. Whenever you are ready, return to normal consciousness.

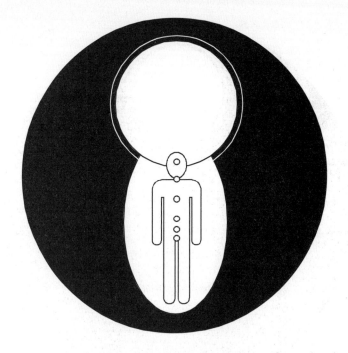

Figure 14. The globe of light reaches the top of your head.

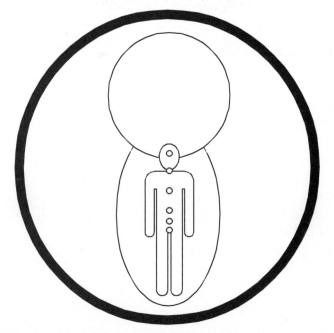

Figure 15. Feel yourself dissolving completely into the light.

Part II

USING THE
NEW HERMETICS

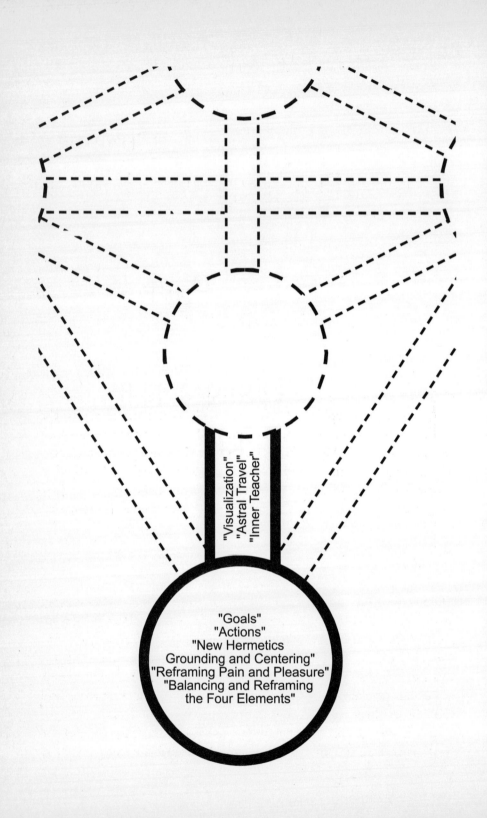

CHAPTER 5
THE INITIATE LEVEL

T he Initiate level of the New Hermetics is a set of tools based upon the sephirah Malkuth (the physical plane of reality, the world of the elements) and the aethyr (your own imagination and subconscious). Most of these tools will introduce you to the basics of exploring your inner world. With them you will begin to look within yourself and to balance the elements of your personality. By using these tools, you will improve your ability to visualize and your ability to understand and manage your internal and your external world.

THE POWER OF GOALS

The first necessary step to succeeding at anything, whether spiritually or in any other area of your life, is to set goals for what you want to accomplish. If you do not know where you are going, you will never get there. The only way to manifest anything is to know specifically what it is you'd like to manifest. By understanding what you want, you will be more able to take the actions necessary to accomplish your goals, and you'll be less likely to do things in opposition to your goals.

It is for this reason that, before you use any more of the tools of the New Hermetics, you must set some goals for yourself. Because the New

Hermetics is a program to help you with all aspects of your life, the goals you set will be in all areas of your life, from the lofty heights of spirituality to other matters such as your financial life and your other material affairs. By looking at all aspects of your life and deciding what you want right now, you will be able to incorporate spiritual technologies into the accomplishment of everything in your life. You deserve happiness and fulfillment on all planes.

As you set goals, please think about what you really want. Don't be afraid to set goals that seem impossible or out of reach. Nothing that you can conceive of is impossible if you really want to make it happen. You are going to be getting in touch with the source of all possibilities and gaining access to infinite power. Please list the goals that will really make you happy and fulfilled. Make sure that your goals are so exciting that you will want to do everything in your power to make them happen. Dare to dream.

The sole reason for doing this exercise is to help you lead a purpose-driven life, a life that makes you happy, fills you with hope and passion, and sustains you in your life's journey. As Joseph Campbell might say, it is to help you "follow your bliss." Please be sure to think about what goals in life would really make you happy. As you get to know yourself better throughout the New Hermetics, these goals will naturally change. That is fine. Discover where you are now.

The New Hermetics separates goals into five categories, corresponding to the four elements, and the fifth element of spirit. These five categories can be separated roughly as follows:

Spirit—Spiritual goals, your life's work.
Fire—Goals for your will, personal power, desires, creativity, and sexuality.
Water—Emotional goals, feelings, and relationships.
Air—Intellectual goals, goals about your ability to communicate.
Earth—Financial goals, physical appearance.

Set four goals in each of these areas, stating each in the positive future tense for now, beginning each statement with, "I will . . ." Figure 16 gives examples of some goals in each category (see figure 16, opposite).

Spirit:
1. I will experience a transcendental union with universal consciousness.
2. I will communicate with Angels.
3. I will radiate love to everyone I meet.
4. I will be an iconoclastic freedom fighter.

Fire:
1. I will feel confident and loving with all people.
2. I will enjoy sex more and more.
3. I will cultivate a high-energy life.
4. I will paint three new paintings.

Water:
1. I will learn to manage my emotional states.
2. I will cultivate a natural state of bliss and peace.
3. I will learn to take things less personally.
4. I will improve my friendships and love life.

Air:
1. I will get my master's degree.
2. I will master my communication with my self and others.
3. I will learn to speak Spanish.
4. I will study more about the Qabala.

Earth:
1. I will earn $200,000 a year in personal income.
2. I will buy new clothes and improve my appearance.
3. I will drive a Corvette.
4. I will become more athletic and lose twenty pounds of fat.

Figure 16. Sample goals organized by element.

Of course, you can set whatever goals you like. Don't be afraid to be as creative and dramatic as you'd like. But please make sure that your goals are things that you really do want. If you set goals that you don't care about, you won't be helping yourself at all. You may always change your goals whenever you want, so just write down what's important to you at the moment. As you grow in all areas of your life, your goals will change and grow as well. You will review your goals often, so you will constantly have the opportunity to change and improve them.

In order to get the most out of anything in your life, it is really necessary to know what it is that you are looking for. Having goals is absolutely essential to accomplishing anything in life. By really knowing what you want, you will be able to get so much more out of the New Hermetics than if you just begin practicing these exercises without any direction. If you take a few moments to decide what you really want, I guarantee that the upcoming exercises will help you to achieve it.

Before you begin writing, I'd like to share with you a few keys that will help make your goals even better than the ones in Figure 16. If you follow these simple rules, your goals will be as effective as possible. They are based on some of the principles of neuro-linguistic programming.

1. State your goals in the positive. Write down what you want, not what you don't want.
2. Make sure your goals are things that you can do. Don't set goals that require others to do things. "I want my girlfriend to stop bugging me," is a poorly formed goal. It will actually disempower you, because you won't be able to guarantee results. "I will figure out how I can get along better with my girlfriend," is something that you can definitely accomplish.
3. State specifically what you want—the amounts, environment—right down to the exact details you want.
4. State your goals in sensory terms. Try not to use vague words such as "enlightenment." State instead that you want to experience ecstasy all through your body and soul and feel an overwhelming sensation of connectedness with everything in the world. This makes your goals something real.
5. State goals in increments or "chunks" that you can believe in. Don't say, "I want to earn a million dollars," say "I'd like to

work every day on improving my financial situation until I achieve the state of abundance in my life."

6. You can put resources into your goals. Create subgoals to give you the abilities to achieve your goal. If you are interested in becoming a successful businesswoman, you will need assertiveness, confidence, focus, perhaps training. Include these factors in your goals.

7. Check the "ecology" of your goals. Make sure that your goals are really something that you want. Is there a part of you that is resistant to the goal? You must address that resistance or you will not succeed.

8. Clarify to yourself what the fulfillment of the goal will be like. Make sure you know specifically how you will know when you've achieved your goal or you may achieve your goal and not even realize it!

Once you have written down your goals in each of the categories, set a time frame for each of them. Do you want to accomplish them in six months, a year, two years, or right now? Write the time frame next to each goal. Once you have done this, choose your five most immediate goals, and think of one thing that you can do right now to begin the process of accomplishing them (see figure 17, page 88). It doesn't have to be a big thing. If you want to learn Spanish, you could buy a book or look into a continuing-education class. If you want to buy a Corvette, you could send away for a brochure.

Now, go out and do these five small things. Don't worry about whether any of your goals are presently financially or emotionally out of reach. Simply begin the process, and you will discover the way to accomplish your goals as you progress in the New Hermetics. Just make sure that you do some small thing to begin the process.

Throughout the New Hermetics, you will return to these goals and make changes in yourself and the world around you with the practices of the New Hermetics that will make it possible to accomplish anything you can dream. This simple exercise will change your life.

You may find it very useful to begin keeping a regular journal of your practice with the New Hermetics tools. Any sort of lined notebook will do. Don't bother purchasing anything too expensive or fancy, as you will feel compelled to record only important things in such a book. Record everything that comes to your mind. By keeping a regular record, you will be able to track your progress and really understand your expanding abilities as they start to blossom. If you don't keep a journal, you won't have any idea where you've been, and that will make it harder to know where you are going. Keep a journal of your thoughts, your actions, and any use of the New Hermetics tools for manifesting magical results. You will learn what is working for you, what is not, and how to change what you are doing to benefit you further in the future. You will discover an incredible amount about yourself and the universe as you proceed. Do not forget to share these things in your journal. You can also download free workbooks for each of the levels of the New Hermetics at *www.newhermetics.com*.

My Five Most Important Goals

1. I will get my master's degree.
     To begin moving toward this goal I will call up the admissions office and get an application.

2. I will buy new clothes and improve my appearance.
     I will make a list of clothing items I need.

3. I will improve my friendships and love life.
     I'm gong to call Gary! I haven't talked to him in ages!

4. I will radiate love to everyone I meet.
     I'm going to smile at ten people today.

5. I will become more athletic and lose twenty pounds of fat.
     I'll ask Gary if he wants to play tennis.

Figure 17. Your five most important goals.

VISUALIZATION POWER

With this simple tool you will begin to improve your abilities to sense things on the inner planes. You will practice the art of visualization as well as learn to smell, taste, hear, and feel in your inner world. You will discover that the easiest way to visualize anything is to simply tell yourself to visualize it, because if you say aloud to yourself in your mind to form a mental image, your unconscious will automatically respond. Consciousness always responds. If you let your unconscious handle the details, it will create exactly what you desire.

1. Enter the altered state as described in chapter 4 (see page 73).
2. Tell yourself verbally in your mind to experience some object. The object will appear visually in your mind, at least for a few moments.
3. As the object appears, begin to imagine what it would be like to experience the object with some of your other senses. You can start with touch, formulating with your mind a set of imaginary hands and allowing yourself to feel the texture of the object. Make this sensation as real as you can.
4. Formulate what it would be like to smell the object.
5. Formulate what it would be like to taste the object.
6. Formulate what sort of sound the object could make.
7. You may repeat this process with as many objects as you like. When you are ready, return to your normal state of awareness.

You may want to try this technique with the following objects in order, because they basically progress in order of complexity and will help you to expand your abilities rapidly.

- A juicy red apple;
- A diamond solitaire ring;
- A beautiful red rose;
- A flaming blue five-pointed star or pentagram;
- A city street, perhaps one that you've been to often;
- A relaxing ocean beach;
- Inside the mouth of a volcano;
- A dog or cat that you know;

- A wild animal such as a lion, a deer, or a wolf;
- A man that you know or a stranger;
- A woman that you know or a stranger;
- A child that you know or a stranger.

You can add as many other things as you can dream up. As you explore this technique, you will discover that one or more of your inner senses or modalities is better developed than others. You may wish to lead with your best-developed inner sense, rather than proceeding in the order in the above exercise. In other words, you may want to start creating inner experiences with your strongest sense, adding the others in order of strength, ending with your weakest sense. Over time, all of your inner senses will improve. Ask yourself the following questions:

1. What sense is easiest to work with, the best-developed inner sense?
2. Which is the next best?
3. Which is the least developed inner sense?

You may also want to try experimenting with eye-accessing, moving your eyes up to the right when visualizing, right and to the side when hearing, and down to the left when feeling (see figure 10, page 54). Again however, each of us is wired differently, so you may have to adjust these directions to make the best use of this.

Practice with this tool a number of times, and eventually you will be capable of imagining objects very vividly. By using the techniques of mentally instructing yourself to experience your inner senses and combining multiple senses, you will find your visualization abilities expanding very rapidly.

YOUR INNER TEMPLE

To use many of the tools of the New Hermetics, you will need a temple or workroom on the inner planes. It is really just a matter of imagining it into existence. This imaginary temple acts as the connecting place between your conscious mind and the endless expanse of the collective unconscious. Now that you have gained a few skills in visualization, you can create this area. It may seem like a silly exercise in imagination for now, but it will grow more and more powerful the more you use your temple. The New Hermetics temple is based on the formula of the tarot card, "The World," with you in the center between the four elemental forces and the greater expanse of the inner universe above you.

You may have already created an inner temple of your own in your previous magical work, and I am in no way trying to replace or supplant that inner temple. However, the inner temple design that follows is specifically for use with the New Hermetics tools, and you will need to create this temple in your inner world in order to get the most out of the New Hermetics. You can certainly continue to use your own inner constructs for other purposes. This temple is merely your New Hermetics inner temple. You can also feel free to "dress up" this temple in any way you like as long as it contains the basic elements outlined below.

1. Enter the altered state as described in chapter 4 (see page 73).
2. Once you are thoroughly relaxed, visualize that you are in a hallway or cave.
3. Move through the hallway, noticing vividly the textures, smells, and sounds.
4. At the end of the hallway, create a door. If you do not see it right away, tell yourself to experience a door and it will appear. This is the entrance to your temple.
5. Open the door and step inside. Visualize your temple as a bare room with four walls, although you may eventually fill it with any objects you want as the need arises.
6. Look at the far wall directly in front of you. This is east in your inner temple. Make this wall yellow with your imagination. This will be the location of the element air. You may visualize this wall more as a window with billowing yellow clouds behind it. Feel a warm breeze, and hear the rustling of wind. Any beings or forces having to do with the element of air will live in and manifest from this wall (see figure 18, page 92).
7. Visualize yourself turning right (clockwise), around to the south wall. Make this wall red. This will be the location of the element fire. You may visualize this wall more as a win-

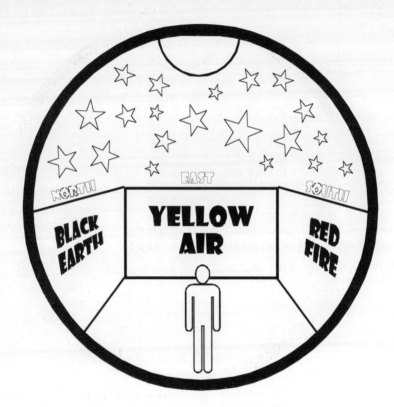

Figure 18. Inner temple, front view.

dow with fiery, red, burning flames behind it. Feel hot
flames, and hear the crackling of fire. Any beings or forces
having to do with the element of fire will live in and manifest from this wall.

8. Visualize yourself turning right (clockwise), around to the
    west wall. You may see the door you came through in this
    wall, but it does not have to be there unless you need it.
    Make this wall blue. This will be the location of the element
    water. You may visualize this wall more as a window with
    flowing, undulating, blue water behind it. Feel the cool
    moisture, and hear the sloshing waves. Any beings or forces
    having to do with the element of water will live in and
    manifest from this wall (see figure 19, opposite).

Figure 19. Inner temple, back view.

9. Visualize yourself turning right (clockwise), around to the north wall. Make this wall black. This will be the location of the element earth. You may visualize this wall more as a window with black crystalline stone formations behind. Feel the cool hardness, and hear the creaking of the earth. Any beings or forces having to do with the element of earth will live in and manifest from this wall.

10. Look up above these walls. Instead of a ceiling, visualize a starry sky. Any beings or forces having to do with the stars or the planets will manifest from above you in this starry expanse.

11. Look directly above your head. Visualize the globe of pure white light from your initiation directly above you. This is

your connection point with cosmic consciousness. It will always be there in your inner temple.

12. Look around at your temple and begin to orient yourself within it. Use all of your inner senses to make it as real for you as possible. This is the place where your magick begins.

13. When you are ready, turn to the western wall and visualize a door. Step through the door back into your usual bodily awareness. Return to normal awareness, knowing that your temple will be there again the next time you need it.

ACTION: THE GATEWAY TO TRANSFORMATION

In order to accomplish anything in life, it is necessary to take action. The goal of the New Hermetics is to help you awaken to your own spiritual power and wisdom and enjoy every aspect of life fully. There are several actions you can take in your day-to-day life that will help you immeasurably on this path. These actions are based on things that you do anyway, but by becoming conscious of them and imbuing them with power, they can immediately increase your personal power and connection to the universe.

This tool is actually four different related actions that you can use every day. They are very easy to accomplish, and will only take you a few seconds to perform. The purpose of these actions is twofold. First, by becoming more conscious of these actions, you will become more conscious of your whole life in general, and this will allow you to see the world more clearly. Second, by placing intention into these everyday actions, you will cause subtle shifts to take place in your life that will be unexpected and beneficial. You can use these tools as often as you like, and you will accumulate force and direction in your life each time you use them.

Conscious Eating

With this tool, you become conscious of what you are eating, increasing your awareness of the immense power in your food. You can then imbue this powerful food with specific intention so that it fortifies you in whatever way you can conceive. The following tools will follow similar procedures with water and breathing.

1. As you sit down to eat a meal, observe the food that is in front of you. Be present with the food and really look at it.
2. Think to yourself about all that has gone into bringing this food to your table—the work of all the people that cultivated, packaged, transported, and provided this food for you. Even more important, think for a moment about the energy from the nutrients in the soil, the sunlight, oxygen, and water that worked together to produce the food, and also the hands that prepared the food, whether yours or someone else's.
3. As you contemplate this, become aware of all the potential power that you will receive when you eat this food. This is a tremendous gift of power from the universe.
4. Now that you are becoming fully aware of the potential power that is in your food, you may consciously decide how you would like this power to be used. With the simple use of your mind, you may charge your food with the task of increasing your vitality, energy, ability to communicate, losing weight, overcoming anxiety, grief, or anger, or any other change or empowerment that you can conceive of and desire for your body/mind.
5. Hold your dominant hand over your food momentarily, and act as if you have the ability to direct the energy of your food. You may make a picture in your mind of a glow or flow of energy; picture a desired outcome, sense a feeling that the energy is moving in the direction you have conceived, just simply tell it to do so verbally in your mind, or some combination. The only important criterion is that you make it as real for you as possible. Create for yourself what it would be like if you had this quality. Imagine what you would see, how you would stand and feel, what you would be saying to yourself.
6. As you eat your food, feel that this transformational energy is flowing into your body and beginning to fill you.
7. When you have completed your meal, thank the universe for the powerful energy that you have received.

Conscious Drinking

With this tool, you become conscious of what you drink, increasing your awareness of its immense power. You can then imbue these liquids with specific intention so that they fortify you in whatever way you can conceive.

1. When you are about to drink a glass of water, become aware of the nature of water, which is cleansing and purifying. Imagine that this water has the magnetic power to remove toxicity and negative energy from both the body and the environment.

2. Imagine that the water is going to purify your body both physically and spiritually as you drink it. Imagine what it would be like if you were purified. Imagine what you would see, how you would stand and feel, what you might be saying to yourself.

3. As you begin to drink the water, feel it flowing through you, drawing toxicity away from you, to remove it from your body as it passes through.

4. When you have finished your glass of water, thank the universe for this cleansing.

Conscious Bathing

Just as water cleanses your insides when you drink it, it draws toxins away from the outside when you bathe. You may want to bathe in cool water, because it is said that the purifying effect of water is reduced when it is hot.

1. As you prepare to bathe, whether showering, taking a bath, or simply washing, become conscious of the purifying power of water.

2. Imagine the water is going to purify you as you bathe. Imagine what it would be like if you were purified. Imagine what you would see, how you would stand and feel, what you would be saying to yourself.

3. As you feel the water running over your skin, imagine all of your physical and spiritual toxins draining away.

4. Visualize, feel, or describe to yourself verbally (or some combination) that toxins are flowing away from you throughout your cleansing.

5. As you dry yourself off, thank the universe for cleansing you so fully.

Conscious Breathing

Breathing is one of our greatest sources of energy and power, but most of us do not even breathe effectively, let alone consciously. By breathing intentionally and deeply, you can quickly give yourself the gift of vitality, energy, tranquility, and any other qualities that you desire. In later tools, you will learn specific, powerful breathing techniques, but for now you will simply learn to breathe with intention, filling your body with power by carrying it on the breath.

1. Become aware of your breathing. Feel it.

2. Breathe slowly and deeply down into your belly, completely filling your lungs. Allow your stomach to expand with your breath.

3. Visualize that the air around you is filled with potentiality for some desired quality that you would like to manifest in your life. For instance, imagine that the air is filled with vitality, courage, strength, intelligence, patience, or whatever you are most in need of at the time. Visualize, feel, or describe to yourself what it would be like if you had this quality. Imagine what you would see, how you would stand and feel, what you would be saying to yourself.

4. With each breath you breathe in, feel this energy entering your lungs and going out into your body through your bloodstream.

5. As you breathe out, feel that the energy is staying behind. Only the breath is going out.

6. Breathe about ten to twenty breaths, visualizing and feeling this desired energy filling your whole body.

7. Thank the universe for the gift of this energy.

Pore Breathing

This tool expands upon the previous tool, enhancing your breathing through the use of the altered state to enable you to experience all your pores as you inhale and exhale. This will enhance your ability to draw in transformative qualities through your breathing.

1. Enter the altered state (see page 73).
2. Breathe slowly and deeply.
3. Feel the sensations on the surface of your skin, as it covers your whole body.
4. Visualize the pores of your skin opening; feeling tingles all over your skin.
5. As you breathe in, visualize and feel the air entering into all of your pores, as well as your lungs, and leaving your pores as you breathe out.
6. Visualize that the air around your body is filled with some desired quality (vitality, healing energy, elemental energy, etc.) You may also feel, hear, or even smell this quality.
7. As you breathe in, feel your whole body filling with this quality through all of your pores.
8. As you breathe out, hold onto the quality inside of you, just letting go of the air.
9. Breathe in about nine more times, filling yourself, charging up like a battery.
10. Continue to breathe normally, feeling the build-up of energy inside of you.
11. Return to normal consciousness.

You may increase the number of breaths to intensify the experience. If you want to release the energy, just let it go while exhaling with the same number of breaths as you breathed in. Later, you will learn to use this energy accumulation in other ways, such as creating artificial elementals, charging spaces, or healing.

You may use these tools as often as you like. The more you use them, the more quickly you will grow as a human being and a New Hermeticist. You may want to concentrate on specific qualities and energies that will help you accomplish the goals you have set for yourself. Concentrating on the same energy repeatedly will help you to manifest it very quickly.

Before we leave the subject of action I must mention a very important action that you should always take, particularly when you are working with the magical tools later on. Whenever you visualize or project any desire out into the universe, you must take some action that will help you to manifest it. In other words, if you create a talisman or an artificial elemental to get yourself a job, look in the paper as soon as possible. If you want to meet a new lover, go out into the world to places where this might happen. If you don't take some action to provide the universe with a clear path for manifesting your desires, you will significantly delay your results. On the other hand, you should not obsess over your desire. Try not to think about your desires at all, or your conscious mind may interfere with fears and doubts. The universe works in peculiar ways. Simply make yourself available and keep your eyes open.

NEW HERMETICS GROUNDING AND CENTERING

This tool is based loosely upon the Lesser Banishing Ritual of the Pentagram of the Hermetic Order of the Golden Dawn.[9] The formula is the same, but the sectarian words of power have been replaced with modern archetypal equivalents. It was originally written by one of my greatest teachers, but she does not wish to be credited. It has been edited, adapted, and incorporated as the official grounding and centering practice of the New Hermetics. The ritual has been reduced to a simple set of mental maneuvers so that it can be conducted quickly, entirely in your inner temple. You may want to practice it physically as a ritual a few times to get a sense of how the movements work, but this isn't entirely necessary. The purpose of this tool is to focus your mind and to put all of the pieces of your consciousness symbolically into their proper places so that you can work most effectively on the inner planes.

1. Enter the altered state (see page 73).
2. Go to your inner temple (see page 90).
3. Stand in the center of your inner temple and look upward.

4. Visualize the globe of brilliant white light above you. Say mentally, "As above . . ."

5. Visualize a beam of white light emanating down from the globe of light to the top of your head. Feel and see this column of light traveling blissfully down through your whole body to your feet.

6. As the column of white light descends down through your feet into the floor of your inner temple, visualize another globe of white light forming at your feet. Say mentally, "So below . . ."

7. Visualize another globe of white light forming by your right shoulder. Say mentally, "In projection . . ."

8. Feel and see another column of light emanating from the globe at your right shoulder, moving through your chest from your right shoulder to your left, and forming a fourth globe

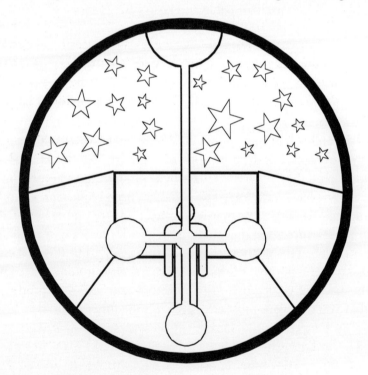

Figure 20. Creating the cross of white light.
As above, so below, in projection, and reflection, one thing.

of light at your left shoulder. Say mentally, "And reflection . . ." You will now have a cross of white light filling your body (see figure 20, opposite).

9. At the center of this cross of light, in your heart, feel and see a golden globe of light form. Feel a sense of bliss emanating from this golden globe in your heart. Say mentally, " . . .one thing" (see figure 20, opposite).

10. Look toward the east of your temple ahead of you, to the yellow wall of air. As you see billowing clouds of yellowish air before you, become aware of the power of your mind, the process of thinking. Visualize a pentagram, and project it at the yellow wall, mentally saying, "Knowledge." As the pentagram reaches the wall, visualize the wall glowing brightly as if you've activated it (see figure 21, page 102). Feel the power of air.

11. Look toward the south of your temple toward your right, to the red wall of fire. As you see burning red flames before you, become aware of your will, your passions and desires. Visualize a pentagram, and project it at the red wall, mentally saying, "Will." As the pentagram reaches the wall, visualize the wall glowing brightly as if you've activated it. Feel the power of fire.

12. Look toward your right, to the west of your temple behind you, the blue wall of water. As you see undulating waves of water before you, become aware of your emotions and feelings. Visualize a pentagram, and project it at the blue wall, mentally saying, "Daring." As the pentagram reaches the wall, visualize the wall glowing brightly as if you've activated it. Feel the power of water.

13. Look toward your right, to the north of your temple, the black wall of earth. As you see rocky structures forming before you, become aware of your plans, your goals, and your physicality. Visualize a pentagram, and project it at the black wall, mentally saying, "Silence." As the pentagram reaches the wall, visualize the wall glowing brightly as if you've activated it. Feel the power of earth.

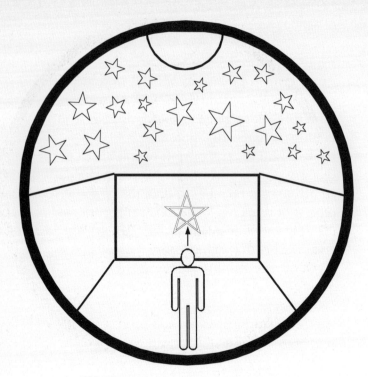

Figure 21. Projecting pentagrams.

14. Look at the yellow eastern wall again, mentally saying, "Before me, intelligence." Visualize a giant golden yellow being forming in the billows of cloud in the east. This is your guardian of the element of air (see figure 22, opposite).
15. Mentally say, "Behind me, understanding." Visualize a giant pulsing blue being forming in the flow of water behind you in the west. This is your guardian of the element of water.
16. Say, "To my right hand, creation." Visualize a giant fiery red being forming in the flames of the south. This is your guardian of the element of fire.
17. Say, "And to my left hand, manifestation." Visualize a giant earthy black being forming among the structures in the north. This is your guardian of the element of earth.
18. Look up once again at the globe of brilliant white light above you. Say mentally,, "As above . . ."

Figure 22. Visualizing guardians.

19. Visualize a beam of white light emanating down from the globe of light to the top of your head. Feel and see this column of light traveling blissfully down through your whole body to your feet.

20. As the column of white light descends down through your feet into the floor of your inner temple, visualize another globe of white light forming at your feet. Say mentally, "So below . . ."

21. Visualize another globe of white light forming by your right shoulder. Say mentally, "In projection . . ."

22. Feel and see another column of light emanating from the globe at your right shoulder, moving through your chest from your right shoulder to your left, and forming a fourth globe of light at your left shoulder. Say mentally, "And reflection . . ." You will now have a cross of white light filling your body.

23. At the center of this cross of light, in your heart, feel and see a golden globe of light. Feel a sense of bliss emanating from this golden globe in your heart. Say mentally, " . . .one thing." Feel and see yourself in the midst of the cross of light and the four elemental powers. At this point, the guardians can fade from your view, so that you can enter the elemental realms as you need to, but they will still be there to protect and empower you.

24. You may return to normal awareness whenever you are ready.

Once you have learned the sequence, this tool can be exercised in just a few moments. By performing this brief operation, you establish the elemental forces of your being in their proper places within your temple and clear away distracting thoughts, feelings, and forces that might otherwise cause you distraction and trouble.

THE FOUR ELEMENTS

As mentioned previously, the four ancient elements correspond very well with certain tendencies of human character. In medieval times, these character traits were called the four humors: the phlegmatic, the sanguine, the melancholic, and the choleric. Even though modern psychology has abandoned this simple model, we all do still possess these character elements within ourselves. With this tool, you will become acquainted with these four elements and begin to understand how they shape your personality. When you begin to understand these subtle forces as they apply to your own personality, you will begin to see imbalances in yourself. These elemental imbalances cause you to act uncontrollably, to be compelled unnecessarily by negative unconscious forces. You will later learn a simple method for addressing these imbalances and returning yourself to a healthy state of equilibrium and free choice. In order to succeed in the New Hermetics, it is necessary to balance your personality so that you are capable of expressing all of the positive traits of each element and not obsessed by any of the negative ones. Return to Figure 3 (page 31) to see personality traits applied to the four elements. With this tool you will discover the elemental imbalances in your current personality.

1. Read the list of personality traits for each element (see figure 3, page 31).
2. Write down in separate columns for each element both the positive and negative qualities of each element that you feel describe you. Add up the positives and negatives from each element, and you will begin to see where your elemental imbalances lie. You will notice that you have more qualities from one or two of the elements than any other.
3. You will also notice that, for nearly every positive quality, you also have at least a tendency toward the negative quality associated with it. However, we all have the potential for all of the positive and negative qualities of all of the elements. We simply have not learned how to access the qualities that we are not used to, and we tend to access the same qualities over and over.
4. In order to balance your personality equation, write down all of the negative qualities of the elements that you are currently experiencing in your life.
5. Write down next to each of these qualities the positive quality from the other element on the same line. In other words, for negative fire qualities, write down the corresponding positive water qualities next to them. For water, write down fire qualities. For air, write down earth qualities. And for earth, write down air qualities.
6. You now have the necessary components for beginning to balance the elements of your personality.

Of course, the lists in Figure 3 do not represent every single character trait. You will most likely need to create further lists with other character traits to take full advantage of the benefits of balancing your personality. These lists are just meant to be indicative, and your own creativity is always much more valuable than simply following my script.

Balancing and Reframing the Elements
With this tool you will be able to move away from negative elemental traits and manifest new positive traits. First, choose from the negative qualities that you really want to discard and the positive qualities that

you'd really like to adopt in your personality. This will help you to succeed with this tool. For example, you may have chosen the negative water trait of "low self-esteem," so the positive fire trait that you will be invoking is "high self-esteem." Using this tool, you will move from low to high self-esteem. Of course, you can use this tool with any negative and positive qualities from Figure 3 or any you've come up with on your own. This tool will allow you to change the way you react to any situation in your life however you may like. It may seem that this technique is very fast and simple, but this is the way your brain changes—quickly and simply.

1. Enter the altered state (see page 73).
2. Go to your inner temple (see page 90).
3. Perform the New Hermetics grounding and centering (see page 99).

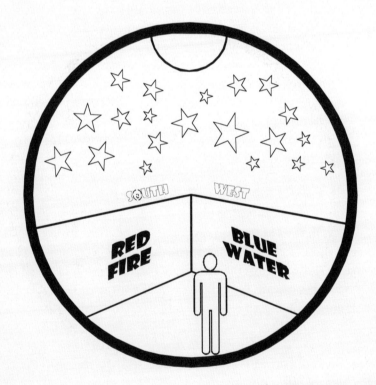

Figure 23. Face the south and west walls when working with fire and water.

4. At the end of the grounding and centering exercise, clear away all images but the blank walls of your temple. Visualize the walls of your temple like blank movie screens where you can project pictures that you will create.

5. Move to the southwest corner of your temple if you are working with fire and water, or the northeast corner if you are working with water and air (see figures 23 and 24, opposite and below). By moving to these positions, you will be straddling the two elemental areas.

6. Turn to the wall corresponding to the negative trait you want to move away from.

7. Make a picture of what you would see through your eyes when you are about to experience this negative trait. Experience whatever feelings, images, or sounds may precede you experiencing your negative trait. Picture it as if you were

Figure 24. Face the north and east walls when working with earth and air.

Figure 25. Face the wall corresponding to your negative trait.

     totally immersed in the experience, seeing what you would
see through your eyes, hearing, feeling the feelings, even
smelling, and then let this image go for a moment (see figure
25, above). Blank this wall of your temple.

8. Turn and look at the wall corresponding to the positive quality you are invoking.

9. Make a bright colorful picture on this wall of what you
would look like when you manifest your new quality (see figure 26, opposite). How will you stand and breathe? What
kind of expression will be on your face? What sorts of new
things will you be able to do? Make this an image of you
looking at yourself in the distance. Make the picture very
appealing and desirable.

10. Shrink this image down so that it is very small and move it
way back into the wall (see figure 27, page 110).

Figure 26. Face the wall corresponding to the positive quality.

11. Look over at the first wall and again visualize, as if through your eyes, an image of the experience that you have just had before when experiencing the negative trait.

12. Quickly shrink this image down to a very small size far away, and turn back to the new positive image on the second wall, saying the magical word, "Swish!" if you like, and making the positive image grow to fill the second wall, brightly and appealingly (see figure 28, page 111). Do this as fast as you can, and then blank both walls.

13. Look over at the first wall and again visualize, as if through your eyes, an image of the experience that you have just had before when experiencing the negative trait.

14. Quickly shrink this image down to a very small size far away, and turn back to the new positive image on the second wall, saying the magical word, "Swish!" and making the positive

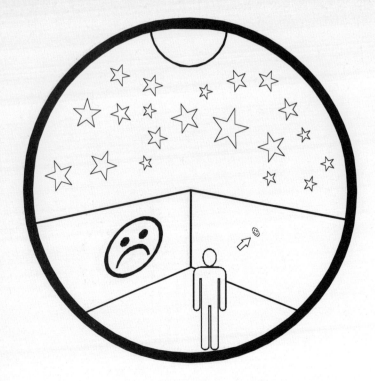

Figure 27. Shrink the positive image down.

image grow to fill the second wall, brightly and appealingly. Do this as fast as you can, and then blank both walls.

15. Repeat this about 10 times as fast as you can, with just a second or two between swishes.

16. Visualize yourself in the future in a situation where, in the past, you would have reacted with the negative trait, and you will discover that the new image instantly pops into your mind. This will allow you the freedom to choose this new trait instead of the old one.

17. Perform the New Hermetics grounding and centering.

18. Return to normal awareness whenever you are ready.

If you ever find yourself slipping back into the old trait in the future, simply use this tool again, and you will find yourself changing forever. You should use this tool with all of your negative traits. It won't really

Figure 28. Shrink the negative image; grow the positive image.

take very long at all, and you will dynamically change yourself into a well-balanced and free individual. Saying "swish" is a tradition in NLP, but is not really necessary, unless you like it.

There is also a much simpler and faster method of accomplishing this same purpose—by moving with the elements physically, feeling and seeing them within you, and allowing yourself to transform in their power. For example, let's say that you are currently more of an earthy personality. You tend to be practical, stable, thorough, but also a little boring and a bit of a perfectionist. And let's say that you would like to be more adventurous, flexible, intellectual, lenient.

To balance this out, all that you need to do is imagine your body filling with the air element. Simply visualize and feel your whole body becoming lighter and filling up with the whirling energy of air. As you do this, imagine that the air carries the character trait that you desire. See it, feel it, hear it vividly inside you.

Then move your body the way it would move if you had this quality. Feel it and experience it inside you. Let it find a home there. Let the imagined element dissolve into the rest of your being. Let yourself experience this new trait as a part of you. Imagine yourself vividly using this new quality in the near future. You may want to repeat this a few times, and you will discover that you have expanded your possibilities permanently in this new direction. The process is exactly the same for all the elements and qualities.

If you want to rid yourself of a negative trait, imagine the appropriate element carrying it away, or imagine the opposite element extinguishing it as you physically move your body in imitation of your inner experience. If you are feeling watery sadness, imagine fire entering, drying up all the water, and filling you instead with fiery passion. Then move about vigorously, feeling the burning intensity driving the motion. Your imagination is the only limit to what you can do with the elements. (See also Appendix 3.)

REFRAMING PAIN INTO PLEASURE

There are experiences in life that we find painful or difficult to deal with. We may retreat from taking action in various parts of our lives because of these pain signals that we receive. These can be totally crippling. However, you can consciously take control of your internal pain and pleasure signals with the use of the following tool.

Simply choose a situation that you experience in your life that currently seems painful, that you would like to become pleasurable, or at least neutral. Follow these steps to change this painful experience into pleasure.

1. Enter the altered state (see page 73).
2. Go to your inner temple (see page 90).
3. Perform the New Hermetics grounding and centering (see page 99).
4. Turn to the left or north of your inner temple, and face the earth wall. See the black color of the wall. Feel the heaviness, hardness, and solidity of the element of earth. Imagine this

wall opening up into a rocky landscape. Step out into this landscape.

5. As you do so, feel yourself becoming one with the element of earth. Become aware of the solidity of your body, your weight and structure. Experience the sensations of stability, composure, and calmness.

6. Become aware of the painful situation, and identify the part of you that creates the pain. Is it a feeling, an image or series of images, or an inner voice telling you something? Once you have found the part of you that causes this pain, establish communication with it, making sure that it is willing to communicate with you.

7. Ask this part of you what the positive intention behind this pain is. This pain is trying to accomplish some useful function, and, if you ask, this part of you will communicate this function. It may do this with a feeling, an image or series of images, or an inner voice telling you something.

8. When you know the positive intention behind this painful experience, ask this part of you if it would be willing to try a different method for achieving the same result, other than giving you this pain. It may say "yes" with a feeling, an image or series of images, or an inner voice telling you something.

9. When you receive a "yes" from this part of you, show this part that it is actually harming you rather than helping you by visualizing three to five situations in which it is causing you pain and making you miss out on pleasure.

10. Connect with your creativity, and come up with three or more alternative ways that this part of you can accomplish the positive intention without causing you pain.

11. Ask this part of you if it will agree to try one or more of these three ways instead of causing you pain.

12. Visualize yourself in the situation that used to cause you pain, and instead allow yourself to feel pleasure. Feel warm, joyful sensations in your body, visualize positive experiences, and tell yourself positive things.

13. Ask the part of you that formerly caused you pain if it will allow you to feel pleasure in this way. If not, go back to step 8 and start again.
14. Make sure that your whole being is comfortable with this change. If not, go back through all of the steps until you feel totally comfortable.
15. Emerge from the earthy landscape to your inner temple.
16. Perform the New Hermetics grounding and centering tool.
17. Return to normal consciousness.

You have successfully reprogrammed your consciousness to experience pleasure where you used to experience pain.

ASTRAL TRAVELING

Strictly speaking, several of the preceding tools have been "astral projections" of a sort, but you may at some point wish to try exploring the world around you in your astral body. This tool will provide you with a simple technique to do just that. It may seem to be merely imagination at first, but by practicing this tool regularly, you may be startled to realize that you've really had an "out-of-body experience." With this tool, you will go through the steps of leaving your body and traveling around outside of it. By repeatedly performing this practice, you will discover that, in fact, you are really leaving your body and entering the subtle planes. For most of the New Hermetics techniques, this tool is unnecessary, because you begin in your inner temple, but this tool may be helpful to you in exploring the true potentialities of your consciousness.

1. Enter the altered state (see page 73).
2. Relax yourself even more deeply, until you feel a sense of lightness or floating. This is unmistakable, and you will be able to get there quite easily if you've followed through the preceding techniques in order.
3. Move your consciousness upward from the base of your spine until it reaches the top of your head, and feel yourself pushing upward and outward.

4. Visualize that the top of your head is a trapdoor, and push this door open.

5. Move out of the top of your head, and look at the room that you're in. You may wish to imagine a shape resembling your body floating above you and move your awareness into this shape. It is okay if this also seems imaginary.

6. Move away from your body, and feel your astral feet on the floor. Start examining the objects in the room around you. Look, touch, hear, smell, taste. Again, this may seem like a mere daydream, but continue pretending.

7. Look down at your astral body, visualizing hands, feet legs, etc.

8. Go out of the room, and look around the rest of the building you are in.

9. You can now go anywhere you wish, simply by willing yourself to move there. Explore. If you go upward, you will experience scenes and beings from the astral plane. You can direct yourself toward specific experiences and places very easily. If you encounter anything unusual, it may be a good idea to go to your inner temple and perform the grounding and centering exercise before returning to your body.

10. Return to normal consciousness.

It may all seem imaginary at first, but you will sometimes discover things that you could not otherwise know. At other times, you will experience things that are not actually real in the physical world. This is the nature of the aethyr. It is not reality, but the place where all possibilities reside. The more often you practice this tool, the more real your experiences will seem and the more really "out-of-your-body" you will become.

MEETING WITH YOUR INNER TEACHER

The purpose of this tool is to provide you with a powerful internal resource for giving you advice on any subject, helping you to understand your internal experiences, and assisting you to remove blocks and end conflicts inside your own inner temple.

Your inner teacher knows everything about you and your universe, because this teacher is a representation in the aethyr of your own connection to cosmic consciousness. You have always had this inner teacher; it is the inner voice that gives you sound advice when you are troubled. Your inner teacher is a real connection with cosmic consciousness, and you will gain tremendously, spiritually and practically, from the use of this technique. You will have access to your inner teacher any time you need assistance through the use of this tool. As you proceed into the future, you can call upon this inner teacher anytime, to help you discover and enhance your creativity, solve problems, and guide you in your inner-temple experiences. To some, this tool may appear to be merely a New Age meditation, but I suggest these readers make a study of ancient Greek magical papyri, where similar techniques are legion.

Communications from your inner teacher may seem to come from your own mind, or they may seem to come from an entirely separate consciousness. You will be able to distinguish the messages of your inner teacher from the rest of your thoughts because they will always be loving and uncritical. Your inner teacher is an excellent resource for accessing internal wisdom any time you are in need. It will be with you at all phases of your New Hermetics work, and you can always call upon this teacher in any situation.

Your inner teacher will also be an excellent resource in solving conflicts with others. When you are working with it to resolve a conflict with someone, tell it about your conflict, and ask what this person symbolizes on the inner plane for you. Your inner teacher will then show you an image or symbolic representation. It may be a being, but it will not resemble the person with whom you are in conflict; rather it is the archetypal energy you are projecting onto them. Then you can ask this figure or symbol if it will communicate with you. When it agrees, ask the figure to tell you how you can get along with it most beneficially; ask it to work with you in the transformation of your life toward the positive. If the figure seems reluctant, hostile, or aggressive, ask it how you can relate more positively to it. Consider any advice you receive, however strange it may appear, and thank the symbolic figure. This is an excellent tool for dissolving conflicts with other people.

Use this tool to meet your inner teacher. Once you are thoroughly familiar with your teacher, you can call him or her anytime, whether you are in your inner temple, on the bus, or at your job. Your inner teacher will be available to help you whenever you're in need.

1. Enter the altered state (see page 73).
2. Go to your inner temple (see page 90).
3. Perform the New Hermetics grounding and centering (see page 99).
4. Look up at the globe of light above you. Visualize a figure in the middle of the light. This is your inner teacher, who has always been there, but you have never noticed before. Allow your teacher's wisdom, love, protection, and acceptance to flow into you. Feel this blissful exchange. Start receiving visual impressions of your teacher. Begin with the feet. Shoes? Bare? Dress? Body fat or thin? Short or tall? What kind of feelings do you get about your teacher? Is your teacher active or passive? Gentle? Extroverted? Your inner teacher will always have this same appearance from now on. It will not be anyone that you know, or any famous figure, historical or fictional. Most likely, the figure's appearance will be vague at first. Do not worry. It is the connection that is important.
5. Ask your inner teacher to take both your hands. Feel this connection. Allow your teacher to give love to you. Allow yourself to feel an intimate connection with your teacher. You may ask your teacher's name, but do not be upset if you cannot hear it today. You will eventually come to know it if it is necessary.
6. Ask your teacher for guidance on any subject that you need to know about or for assistance in removing any blocks or problems in your life. Allow images and insights to be exchanged between you and your teacher. If you do not understand any messages that come to you, ask for them to be clarified, and they will be.
7. When you have finished communicating with your teacher, thank it and make sure it will be available when you need advice. You will be assured of this.
8. Perform the New Hermetics grounding and centering.
9. Return to normal consciousness.

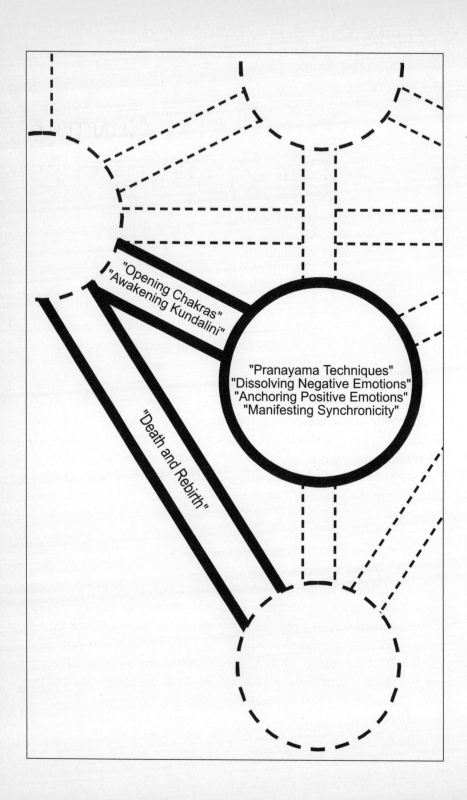

CHAPTER 6

THE ZEALOT LEVEL

The Zealot level of instruction explores your emotional world. The purpose of these tools is to help you understand and develop your emotional body to empower you with greater energy and freedom in all areas of your life. You will learn a number of techniques for changing your emotional states and a number of breathing and focusing techniques that make it possible to clear yourself of negative emotions and fill yourself with energy.

DEATH AND REBIRTH

The Zealot level begins with an exploration of death and reawakening into eternal, spiritual life. This is a tool for rebirth into a higher life, an awakening into a higher level of being. Before you can truly experience higher consciousness in a practical way, you must overcome the fear of death. This tool helps you overcome this fear and become aware of the eternity in which we all dwell. Go through these steps several times to get full benefit from this tool. It is one of the more complicated tools, with a number of separate pieces.

1. Enter the altered state (see page 73).
2. Go to your inner temple (see page 90).
3. Perform the New Hermetics grounding and centering (see page 99).
4. Turn to the back of your temple. This is the western wall, the wall of water. Visualize a hallway opening up before you, making a path between the waters, a path to your possible future, to the end of your life.
5. As you move along this path, visualize a door off to the left. Open the door, feeling its weight, and step through. There are three basic ways you can imagine your death. You can use any of these, or all three on different occasions.

    • Visualize a person who looks just like you suffering from a crippling disease. Move toward and become one with this person, seeing through their eyes, feeling their pains and sensations, hearing their desperate thoughts. Feel the exhaustion of this person's disease. Know that you only have moments left to live. Feel a darkness growing in your entire being, take your final breath, and feel your body and consciousness fading into blackness.

    • Visualize a person that looks just like you, healthy and vibrant, walking down the street in the town where you live. Move forward and become one with this person, seeing through their eyes, feeling their footsteps, hearing the sounds of the street. Begin to feel a sense of dread as you realize that this person is about to have a terrible accident. You may begin to realize what sort of accident this will be—a car accident, a terrible fall, something crushing this person, or a physical attack. Know that this is only moments away. See the cause of the accident ahead of you, approaching, and know that there is nothing to be done to prevent it. It is too late. You cannot get away. Feel this person's body assaulted cruelly, their blood and fluids spilling out, bones crushing, and see a red film over your eyes as life fades and this person's body is limp and twisted, wounds pulsing and burning. As your vision fades to black, the pain diminishes, until you're in blackness and feel nothing.

- Visualize a very ancient person that looks just like you will, having lived a long and complete life—perhaps eighty or ninety years old. See this person lying in bed, surrounded by people who love them. Hear the people giving this person love and saying goodbye in their own special way. Become one with this person, seeing through their eyes and feeling their great tiredness. Hear the messages of love from the people all around. Realize that this person is about to die. See the people around you, both sad and happy to be spending your last moments with you. Take your final breath, and feel life leave you. Your breath seems to be gone. Your heartbeat seems to be gone, but you are still in the body of this person.

6. See yourself now in an unusual place. It is a temple, and you are surrounded by what seem to be Egyptian priests. Visualize that one of them cuts open your midsection with a long ceremonial knife, though you don't feel any physical pan. See several more priests joining him at your open midsection, removing your internal organs, and placing them into ceramic jars.

7. Visualize them placing herbs and salts into your empty body cavity. They rub your lifeless body head to foot in a sticky substance and wrap your body up with long strips of linen. They cover your whole body and then place you into a sarcophagus. You hear the scraping of a large slab of stone as it slides above you, sealing you in blackness.

8. Feel the sensation of breath entering your nostrils, and feel that it is the breath of eternity. See a light entering your eyes, filling them with brightness. Hear a voice or chorus awakening your ears sweetly. Feel an eternal kiss pressing love into your lips and a divine energy coursing down from your lips through your body. As it reaches your reproductive organs, it courses out of you, surrounding you with an egg of brilliant light. You discover that this auric egg is becoming one with the Sun. See and feel the brightness of the Sun within and around you. Let this last only a few moments, then see darkness all around you once again.

9. In the darkness, visualize a gateway. Pass through the gateway, and visualize millions of naked people, writhing with

one another, still trying to enjoy the pleasures of the body. But they no longer have real bodies, and you can tell that there is no pleasure for them, only the memory of pleasure. Move past them quickly and visualize another gateway.

10. As you pass through this gate, see thousands of people prostrating themselves in worship. You can see the intensity of their worship, but you cannot see what they are worshipping. They don't seem to be worshipping anything. Move quickly past these bodies and visualize another gate.

11. Pass through this gate and visualize hundreds of bodies pondering the eternal. You can see their mental struggles, but you can also see that they find no answers, so move on and visualize another gateway.

12. Passing through this gateway, see less than twenty bodies, perfectly still in postures of meditation. They seem very calm, as if they are frozen in their contemplation. Move on, visualizing another gateway.

13. As you pass through, you find that there is no place beyond this gateway. See only a pure soft light and feel yourself growing and dissolving, feeling a connection with everything in the universe. Say to yourself:

My hair is the hair of eternity.
My face is the face of eternity.
My eyes are the eyes of eternity.
My ears are the ears of eternity.
My nose is the nose of eternity.
My lips are the lips of eternity.
My teeth are the teeth of eternity.
My neck is the neck of eternity.
My shoulders are the shoulders of eternity.
My arms are the arms of eternity.
My spine is the spine of eternity.
My sex organs are the sex organs of eternity.
My sinews are the sinews of eternity.
My chest is the chest of eternity.
My belly is the belly of eternity.

My buttocks are the buttocks of eternity.
My legs are the legs of eternity.
My feet are the feet of eternity.
My bones are the bones of eternity.
There is no part of me that is not a part of eternity!

After you feel this oneness with eternity for a time, re-materialize, returning to you inner temple, and thank the universe for whatever experience you have had.

14. Perform the New Hermetics grounding and centering.
15. Return to normal consciousness.

DISSOLVING NEGATIVE EMOTIONS

Negative emotions lodge themselves in our bodies and make it difficult for us to enjoy life fully. These emotions are actually trying to help us change negative patterns in our lives, but we often repress these messages. The negative emotions then linger in some place of tightness in our bodies. Emotions are meant to move through us, like the ebbs and flows of the sea. When we try to avoid or ignore our difficult emotions, they become stuck and can harm us and block us from our true potential. It is important to use this tool in conjunction with understanding the message that the emotion is giving to us, and to listen to its advice. It is only then that you can really let the emotion flow through and away from you fully.

There are essentially two ways of moving past negative emotions. You can either shift the focus of your awareness, allowing the emotion to dissipate, or change your body's physiology in some way that allows the emotion to dissolve.

Changing Your Emotions by Changing Physiology

There are three components to changing your emotions with your physiology:

- Changing your posture or body position;
- Changing your breathing pattern;
- Changing your facial expression.

These components can be used individually or in combination. The New Hermetics tool uses all three together.

1. Notice a negative emotion that you are experiencing—sadness, fear, depression, anger, doubt. It will likely be a feeling, but it may also be connected with images or inner voices. As this emotion comes into your awareness, discover the positive intention behind it—to alert you to danger, a problem, to inform you that you don't like something or that you are involved in an unhealthy situation. To do this, simply be present with the emotion, feeling where it is in your body, and what it is signaling to you. You may experience an image or inner voice. When you know the purpose of the emotion, you no longer need to be held back by it.

2. Move your awareness to the place where you feel the emotion is stuck. This will be a feeling of tension somewhere. Move your body into a new position, opening up this area of tension and allowing it to relax. Move your body as dramatically as you like; the more dramatically you move it, the faster the negative feeling can dissolve. You may even want to shake your body or wave your arms.

3. Take several deep breaths, allowing the emotion to move.

4. Change your facial expression by smiling and opening your eyes wide.

5. The emotion will now move through you, so you may decide with a clear mind what course of action you should take to address the source of the negative emotion.

6. Act immediately to address this issue, to solve the problem or communicate the situation that caused the negative emotion—at least communicating to yourself.

Changing Emotions by Changing Mental Focus

This tool is particularly useful for negative emotions that seem to have non-physical components—negative voices in your head, unpleasant images or memories that hold you back.

1. Notice a negative emotion that you are experiencing—sadness, fear, anger, doubt. As this emotion comes into your awareness, discover the positive intention behind this emotion—to alert you to danger, a problem, to inform you that you don't like something or that you are involved in an unhealthy situation. Simply be present with the emotion, feeling what it is signaling to you.

2. Observe how this negative emotion is manifesting. Is it visual—a negative image? Is it auditory—a discouraging or negative voice, your own or another's? Is it kinesthetic—a negative feeling in your body? Are there several components?

3. Now observe the submodalities or specific qualities of your experience. If it's an image, how big or bright is it? Is it in color or black and white? Is it near or far? If it's auditory, what is the quality of the sound or voice? If it's a feeling, what type of feeling? Sharp or dull? Constant or throbbing?

4. Now begin to experiment with changing some of the submodalities of this negative emotional experience so that it seems less unpleasant. If it is a big, bright image, make it smaller and more dull. If you hear a harsh negative voice, try turning it into a soothing or comical one. If it is a sharp negative feeling, adjust it into a pleasurable or erotic sensation.

5. Change the context of this emotion by really thinking about the fact that it is trying to help or to teach you something important.

6. The emotion will now move through you, so you may decide with a clear mind what course of action you should take to address the source of the negative emotion.

7. Act immediately to address this issue, to solve the problem or communicate the situation, at least communicating to yourself.

These two tools can also be used together to enhance the power of both.

ANCHORING POSITIVE EMOTIONS

Anchors are one of the ultimate weapons for the New Hermeticist. We will literally create signals for our emotional bodies to shift automatically in a new direction. You can easily adapt the following tool to anchor any emotional state, but with this tool, you will at least create anchors for the following positive emotions: creativity, tranquility, vitality, excellent communication, instant meditation, instant confidence.

The anchors will be attached to finger signals that are based on some ancient hand gestures from both the Tantric and the Hermetic magical traditions, and they will be extremely powerful in helping you to literally transform your life.

Creativity

1. Enter the altered state (see page 73).
2. Go to your inner temple and perform the New Hermetics grounding and centering (see pages 90 and 99).
3. You should now be in a passive and neutral state, alert and relaxed. Recall a specific time when you felt totally creative, whether in the arts, business, writing, or problem-solving. If you cannot think of any time that you were creative, simply imagine what it would be like if you were, or think of someone who you think really is. You can even physically move your body into the position it would be in if you were in a creative state. Experience the things you would be seeing, hearing, or saying to yourself, and the feelings in your body in this creative state. Become totally immersed in this experience of creativity. Turn up all of the submodalities so that you are totally involved in this state of creativity. When this reaches a peak and you feel you are really "there," press your index fingers and thumbs together firmly and say to yourself, "creativity" (see figure 29, opposite).
4. Again, vividly create the state of creativity in your body— your breathing, images, sounds, feelings—and at the peak, press your index fingers and thumbs together firmly and say to yourself, "creativity."
5. Repeat this several times.
6. Go back into a neutral state and test your anchor. Press your fingers and thumbs together firmly in the same way you did before, and say to yourself, "creativity." You should automatically experience the sensations, images, and physiology of

creativity snapping back into your consciousness. If they do not, repeat steps 3-5 until they do.

7. Perform the New Hermetics grounding and centering and return to normal conscious awareness.

You have now created instant access to your creativity. Whenever you are in need, you can return to a creative state of consciousness simply by using this anchor.

Tranquility

1. Enter the altered state (see page 73).
2. Go to your inner temple and perform the New Hermetics grounding and centering (see pages 90 and 99).
3. You should now be in a passive and neutral state, alert and relaxed. Recall a specific time when you felt totally tranquil, relaxed in all parts of your being. If you cannot think of any time that you were tranquil, simply imagine what it would be like if you were, or think of someone who you think really is. Experience the things you would see, hear, and feel in

Figure 29. Index fingers and thumbs together signal creativity.

your body in this tranquil state. Become totally immersed in this experience of tranquility. Turn up all of the submodalities so that you are totally involved in this state of tranquility. When this reaches a peak and you feel you are really "there," press your middle fingers and thumbs together firmly and say to yourself, "tranquility" (see figure 30, below).

4. Again, vividly create the state of tranquility in your body— your breathing, images, sounds, feelings—and at the peak, press your middle fingers and thumbs together firmly and say to yourself, "tranquility."

5. Repeat this several times.

6. Go back into a neutral state and test your anchor. Press your middle fingers and thumbs together firmly in the same way you did before, and say to yourself, "tranquility." You should automatically experience the sensations, images, and physiology of tranquility snapping back into your consciousness. If they do not, repeat steps 3-5 until they do.

7. Perform the New Hermetics grounding and centering and return to normal conscious awareness.

Figure 30. Middle fingers and thumbs together signal tranquility.

You have now created instant access to your tranquility. Whenever you are in need, you can return to a tranquil state of consciousness simply by using this anchor.

Vitality
1. Enter the altered state (see page 73).
2. Go to your inner temple and perform the New Hermetics grounding and centering (see pages 90 and 99).
3. You should now be in a passive and neutral state, alert and relaxed. Recall a specific time when you felt totally vital, vibrant, and energetic—a time when you were just flowing, beaming, and really excited about life. If you cannot think of any time that you were vital, simply imagine what it would be like if you were, or think of someone who you think really is. You may want to physically move your body into the position it would be in if you were in a vital state. Experience the things you would be seeing, hearing, or saying to yourself, and the feelings in your body in this vital state. Become totally emotionally involved in this experience of vitality. Turn up all of the submodalities so that you are totally involved in this state of vitality. When this reaches a peak and you feel you are really "there," press your ring fingers and thumbs together firmly and say to yourself, "vitality" (see figure 31, page 130).
4. Again, vividly create the state of vitality in your body—your breathing, images, sounds, and feelings—and at the peak, press your ring fingers and thumbs together firmly and say to yourself, "vitality."
5. Repeat this several times.
6. Go back into a neutral state and test your anchor. Press your fingers and thumbs together firmly in the same way you did before, and say to yourself, "vitality." You should automatically experience the sensations, images, and physiology of vitality snapping back into your consciousness. If they do not, repeat steps 3-5 until they do.
7. Perform the New Hermetics grounding and centering and return to normal conscious awareness.

Figure 31. Ring fingers and thumbs together signal vitality.

You have now created instant access to your vitality. Whenever you are in need, you can return to a vital state of consciousness simply by using this anchor.

Excellent Communication

1. Enter the altered state (see page 73).
2. Go to your inner temple and perform the New Hermetics Grounding and Centering (see pages 90 and 99).
3. You should now be in a passive and neutral state, alert and relaxed. Recall a specific time when you felt totally communicative, a time when you were able to get your ideas across clearly and connect with others. If you cannot think of any time that you were really communicating well, simply imagine what it would be like if you were, or think of someone who you think really can. You can even physically move your body into the position it would be in if you were in a totally communicative state. Experience the things you would be

Figure 32. Pinky fingers and thumbs together signal communication.

seeing, hearing, or saying to yourself, and the feelings in your body in this communicative state. Become totally emotionally involved in this experience of communication. Turn up all of the submodalities so that you are totally involved in this state of communication. When this reaches a peak and you feel you are really "there," press your pinky fingers and thumbs together firmly and say to yourself, "communication" (see figure 32, above).

4. Again, vividly create the state of communication in your body—your breathing, images, sounds, and feelings—and at the peak, press your pinky fingers and thumbs together firmly and say to yourself, "communication."

5. Repeat this several times.

6. Go back into a neutral state and test your anchor. Press your fingers and thumbs together firmly in the same way you did before, and say to yourself, "communication." You should automatically experience the sensations, images, and physiol-

ogy of communication snapping back into your consciousness. If they do not, repeat steps 3-5 until they do.
7. Perform the New Hermetics grounding and centering and
   return to normal conscious awareness.

You have now created instant access to your excellent communication.
Whenever you are in need, you can return to a communicative state of
consciousness simply by using this anchor.

Instant Meditation

This tool is particularly important to the New Hermetics. You will use
this anchor to enter the altered state of consciousness from now on.

1. Enter the altered state (see page 73).
2. Go to your inner temple and perform the New Hermetics
   grounding and centering (see pages 90 and 99).
3. You should now be in a passive and neutral state, alert and
   relaxed. Allow yourself to deepen your relaxation to the
   deepest that you can while continuing to focus. You may do
   this by progressive relaxation, or simply by allowing yourself
   to drift deeper and deeper. When you reach this very deep
   state of relaxation, extremely internal, feeling very light or
   heavy, as if you are barely in your body, observe the sensations, images, and sounds you are hearing. When you reach a
   peak and you feel you are really "there," press your index fingers, your middle fingers, and your thumbs together firmly
   and say to yourself, "altered state" (see figure 33, opposite).
4. Again, vividly create the state of deep relaxation and concentration in your body—your breathing, images, sounds, feelings—and at the peak, press your index fingers, middle fingers,
   and thumbs together firmly and say to yourself, "altered state."
5. Repeat this several times.
6. Go back into a neutral state and test your anchor. Press your
   fingers and thumbs together firmly in the same way you did
   before, and say to yourself, "altered state." You should automatically experience the sensations, images, and physiology

Figure 33. Index, middle fingers, and thumbs together signal meditation.

of the altered state snapping back into your consciousness. If they do not, repeat steps 3-5 until they do.

7. Perform the New Hermetics grounding and centering and return to normal conscious awareness.

You have now created instant access to your altered state of consciousness. From now on, you can return to the altered state for New Hermetics tools or any kind of meditation or trance work simply by using this anchor. You will notice that you are using the previous anchors for tranquility and creativity together. As you might guess, this stacking of anchors is totally intentional, because tranquility and creativity are both prerequisite to meditation.

Instant Confidence

1. Enter the altered state using your meditation anchor (see above).
2. Go to your inner temple and perform the New Hermetics grounding and centering (see pages 90 and 99).
3. You should now be in a passive and neutral state, alert and relaxed. Recall a specific time when you felt totally confident,

whether in the arts, business, writing, or problem-solving. If you cannot think of any time that you were confident, simply imagine what it would be like if you were, or think of someone who you think really is. You can even physically move your body into the position it would be in if you were in a confident state. Experience the things you would be seeing, hearing, or saying to yourself, and the feelings in your body in this confident state. Become totally emotionally involved in this experience of confidence. Turn up all of the submodalities so that you are totally involved in this state of confidence. When this reaches a peak and you feel you are really "there," press your ring fingers, pinky fingers and thumbs together firmly and say to yourself, "confidence" (see figure 34, opposite).

4. Again, vividly create the state of confidence in your body—your breathing, images, sounds, feelings—and at the peak, press your ring fingers, pinky fingers, and thumbs together firmly and say to yourself, "confidence."

5. Repeat this several times.

6. Go back into a neutral state and test your anchor. Press your fingers and thumbs together firmly in the same way you did before, and say to yourself, "confidence." You should automatically experience the sensations, images, and physiology of confidence snapping back into your consciousness. If they do not, repeat steps 3-5 until they do.

7. Perform the New Hermetics grounding and centering and return to normal conscious awareness.

You have now created instant access to your confidence. Whenever you are in need, you can return to a confident state of consciousness simply by using this anchor. You will again notice that you are using the previous anchors for vitality and communication together. As before, this stacking of anchors is totally intentional, because these qualities are both prerequisite to confidence.

You can use this same basic pattern to create instant access to any state you like. You will need to create different triggers for each one, but

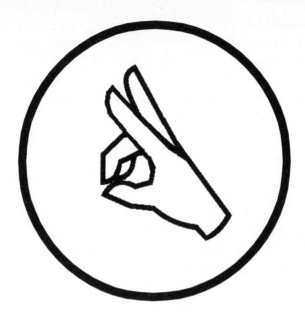

Figure 34. Ring fingers, pinky fingers, and thumbs
together signal confidence.

these can really be anything from other hand signals to touching various parts of your body or anything that seems appropriate to you.

PRANAYAMA

One of the most effective ways to cleanse and calm your emotional body
is through the breath. The next few tools offer breathing techniques
that are based on Eastern yoga practices. This is one of the only parts of
the New Hermetics that specifically uses Eastern technology. The reason
for this is that the yogis of India have a very scientific understanding of
the emotional body and specific techniques for centering and managing
the emotions. We are borrowing these techniques because of their practical value. The ancient Hermetic tradition most likely contained some
similar breath technologies, but they are unfortunately lost to history.

Please keep in mind the Western breathing tools you were taught at
the Initiate level, because you will be able to use the technology of charging
the breath energy with intention during your pranayama once you are
familiar with these techniques.

Do not use these tools within an hour after eating, as it may cause abdominal discomfort. If at any time you are feeling excessively uncomfortable, please stop and resume again later. The purpose of these tools is to purify, vitalize, and calm your body, not to make you ill. If you are in a state of ill health, use these tools with caution and build up slowly.

Pranayama 1—Complete Yogic Breath

This tool will dramatically increase the oxygen supply in your body. It will allow your heart rate to slow down, calming your body and allowing your central nervous system to relax.

1. Sit down in a place where your spine can remain comfortably straight and erect.
2. Enter the altered state using your meditation anchor (see page 132).
3. Take a deep breath through your nostrils, and as you let it out, pull your abdomen inward and upward, fully emptying your lungs.
4. Inhale deeply, drawing the air down into your belly, allowing your abdomen to open up.
5. Continue to breathe air in fluidly, allowing your ribcage to open, and allow the air to fill your lungs all the way up to your collarbone. Your entire lung capacity should be comfortably full.
6. Hold this breath for a brief moment, then release it slowly through your nostrils, starting at the upper chest, and finally completely emptying the belly, gently drawing your abdomen inward to let out all of your breath. This is one complete breath.
7. Repeat this breathing pattern ten to twenty times.

Pranayama 2—Kapalabhati Breath

This tool is somewhat similar to the last, but slightly more vigorous. The purpose of this exercise is to cleanse the respiratory system, to invigorate the body, to clear the mind, and to improve your concentration. It also tones the stomach, heart, and liver. If you are in poor physical condition, you may wish to reduce the number of repetitions to five or ten.

1. Sit down in a place where your spine can remain comfortably straight and erect.
2. Enter the altered state using your meditation anchor (see page 132).
3. Take a deep breath through your nostrils and, as you let it out, pull your abdomen inward and upward slowly, fully emptying your lungs.
4. Inhale deeply as before, drawing the air down into your belly, allowing your abdomen to open up, allowing your ribcage to open, and allowing the air to fill your lungs all the way up to your collarbone. Your entire lung capacity should be comfortably full.
5. As your lungs reach their full capacity, vigorously and quickly exhale through your nostrils, pulling in your abdomen to empty your lungs completely.
6. Repeat this breathing pattern twenty times, then take a complete breath and hold it in as long as possible. Let this breath out naturally. Resume normal breathing.

Pranayama 3—Anuloma Viloma Breath

This is alternate-nostril breathing. The purpose of this tool is to align the right and left sides of your body, so that energy flows evenly through it. As you breathe with this exercise, use a ratio of 1:4:2 for inhaling: retaining: exhaling. In the instructions, we use the count of 4:16:8, but you can adjust this to your personal needs and level of experience. It is said that you begin to develop *siddhis*, or magical powers such as levitation, when you retain the breath for a minute or more, but you'll have to experiment to find out for yourself. You may notice some unusual physical phenomena such as bodily rigidity, perspiration, and feeling lighter than air as a result of using this tool. If you are left-handed, you may reverse these instructions as you see fit.

1. Sit down in a place where your spine can remain comfortably straight and erect.
2. Enter the altered state using your meditation anchor (see page 132).

3. With your right hand, curl your index and middle fingers down to your palm, so your thumb, ring, and pinky fingers remain outstretched. Bring your right hand up to your nose.
4. Breathe in through your left nostril, closing your right nostril with your thumb as you count from 1 to 4.
5. Hold your breath for a count of 16, closing both nostrils with your thumb and fingers.
6. Breathe out through the right nostril, closing your left with your ring and pinky fingers, counting to 8.
7. Breathe in through your right nostril, continuing to close your left nostril with your ring and pinky fingers as you count from 1 to 4.
8. Hold your breath for a count of 16, closing both nostrils with your thumb and fingers.
9. Breathe out through the left nostril, closing your right with your thumb, counting to 8.
10. Repeat this sequence between five and twenty times.
11. Return to normal awareness.

Pranayama 4—Clearing Blocks in the Energy System of the Chakras
With this tool, you will explore the seven chakras through breathing into them and working with your inner teacher to remove any blocks that may be there. With this tool, you will physically learn the location of each of your chakras, begin to explore the feelings associated with each, and start to clear blocks in your energy system to allow the free flow of *kundalini* through your system.

By regularly stimulating your chakras with this and the next tool, you will increase your overall inner energy level, evolve more rapidly, and get more joy and bliss out of life. Your inner teacher can help you to understand and to clear any blocks that you may find in your chakras.

To "breathe energy into" your chakras, simply imagine that, as you are breathing, you are pulling breath vibrations. You can use imaginary hands to open your chakras while you are in the altered state. Imagine you are pulling open two flaps of skin or the petals of a flower at the site of your chakra. Try to feel this without tensing your muscles. Figure 35 (opposite) illustrates the process.

1. Sit down in a place where your spine can remain comfortably straight and erect.

2. Enter the altered state by using your meditation anchor (see page 132). You may contact your inner teacher at any time if you need help.

3. Breathe relaxing energy up from your feet to your base chakra, your *mulhadhara*, which means "root support." This center is at the base of your spine. Feel for a sensation in this area, until you discover some internal kinesthetic experience. Visualize a set of imaginary hands, and use them to pull open this area. Feel a sensation as if you are opening an orifice. Feel any emotions that are in this area, be with them non-judgmentally; and let them flow. Ask your inner teacher to help you understand and remove any blocks that you may experience. Pull energy up from your feet and fill the chakra.

4. Breathe energy up through from your feet, through the base chakra, and on up to the sex chakra, *svadisthana*, which means "her special abode." This center is at the base of your genitals. Feel for a sensation in this area, until you discover

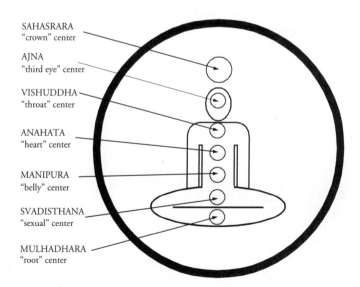

SAHASRARA
"crown" center

AJNA
"third eye" center

VISHUDDHA
"throat" center

ANAHATA
"heart" center

MANIPURA
"belly" center

SVADISTHANA
"sexual" center

MULHADHARA
"root" center

Figure 35. The seven chakras.

some internal kinesthetic experience. Visualize a set of imaginary hands, and use them to pull open this area. Feel a sensation as if you are opening an orifice. Feel any emotions that are in this area, be with them non-judgmentally, and let them flow. Ask your inner teacher to help you understand and remove any blocks that you may experience. Pull energy up from your feet and fill the chakra.

5. Breathe energy up from your feet, through the base and sex chakras and on up to the solar plexus chakra, the *manipura*, which means "city of the shining jewel." This center is somewhere in the area between the bottom of your navel and the top of your solar plexus. Feel for a sensation in this area, until you discover some internal kinesthetic experience. Visualize a set of imaginary hands, and use them to pull open this area. Feel a sensation as if you are opening an orifice. Feel any emotions that are in this area, be with them non-judgmentally, and let them flow. Ask your inner teacher to help you understand and remove any blocks that you may experience. Pull energy up from your feet and fill the chakra.

6. Breathe energy up from your feet, through the base, sex, and solar plexus chakras and on up to the heart chakra, your *anahata*, which means "not struck." This center is in the area of your heart. Feel for a sensation in this area, until you discover some internal kinesthetic experience. Visualize a set of imaginary hands, and use them to pull open this area. Feel a sensation as if you are opening an orifice. Feel any emotions that are in this area, be with them non-judgmentally, and let them flow. Ask your inner teacher to help you understand and remove any blocks that you may experience. Pull energy up from your feet and fill the chakra.

7. Breathe energy up from your feet, through the base, sex, solar plexus, and heart chakras to the throat chakra, *vishuddha*, which means "purified." This center is somewhere at the front of your throat. Feel for a sensation in this area, until you discover some internal kinesthetic experience. Visualize a set of imaginary hands, and use them to pull open this area. Feel a sensation as if you are opening an orifice. Feel any

emotions that are in this area, be with them non-judgmentally, and let them flow. Ask your inner teacher to help you under-stand and remove any blocks that you may experience. Pull energy up from your feet and fill the chakra.

8. Breathe energy up from your feet, through the base, sex, solar plexus, heart, and throat chakras to the brow chakra, third eye, or *ajna*, which means "command." This center is between your two eyes. Feel for a sensation in this area, until you discover some internal kinesthetic experience. Visualize a set of imaginary hands, and use them to pull open this area. Feel a sensation as if you are opening an orifice. Feel any emotions that are in this area, be with them non-judgmen-tally, and let them flow. Ask your inner teacher to help you understand and remove any blocks that you may experience. Pull energy up from your feet and fill the chakra.

9. Draw energy up, as in the previous steps, to the crown chakra, the *sahasrara*, which means "thousand-petaled." This center is at the very top of your head. Feel for a sensation in this area, until you discover some internal kinesthetic experi-ence. Visualize a set of imaginary hands, and use them to pull open this area. Feel a sensation as if you are opening an orifice. Feel any emotions that are in this area, be with them non-judgmentally, and let them flow. Ask your inner teacher to help you understand and remove any blocks that you may experience. Pull energy up from your feet and fill the chakra.

10. At this point, just be with the flow of energy through you, feeling the energy flowing naturally and freely.

11. Then close each of the chakras with your imaginary hands and return to normal consciousness.

Pranayama 5—Charging Chakras with Seed Mantras and Circulating Energy

With this tool, you will begin to charge your chakras with the resonant energy of specific "seed" sounds that the ancient yogis discovered as they meditated. By intoning these sounds, you will be helping your chakras to vibrate at their most effective natural frequencies (see figure 36, page

143). This may or may not be literally true, but it seems to have a salutary effect either way.

You will also visualize a color of the rainbow in each of your chakras. This is a modern New Age addition to working with the chakras, but it does seem to have a valuable and transformative effect on your inner visualization of the chakras and the flow of kundalini energy. This tool may seem a little complicated at first, but it is really quite simple once you get used to it.

1. Sit down in a place where your spine can remain comfortably straight and erect.

2. Enter the altered state using your meditation anchor (see page 132).

3. Move your attention to your base, or *mulhadhara*, chakra. Open this area with imaginary hands. Exhale completely, then slowly fill your lungs to a count of four, imagining that the breath is filling this chakra, and mentally saying, "Lam, Lam, Lam, Lam." (This is the seed mantra for the *mulhadhara* chakra, as the following are the seed sounds for the rest.) As you are breathing in, and intoning "Lam," visualize and feel this area being filled with a bright red energy. Retain your breath for sixteen counts, mentally saying "Lam" with each count, visualizing and feeling the energy brightening and vibrating. Exhale, verbally saying "Lam" for eight counts. Repeat this process four times.

4. Move your attention to your sex, or *svadisthana*, chakra. Open this area with imaginary hands. Exhale completely, then slowly fill your lungs to a count of four, imagining that the breath is filling this chakra, and mentally saying "Vam, Vam, Vam, Vam." As you breathe in and intone "Vam," visualize and feel this area being filled with a bright orange energy. Retain your breath for sixteen counts, mentally saying "Vam" with each count, visualizing and feeling the energy brightening and vibrating. Exhale, verbally saying "Vam" for eight counts. Repeat this process four times.

5. Move your attention to your belly, or *manipura*, chakra. Open this area with imaginary hands. Exhale completely,

then slowly fill your lungs to a count of four, imagining that the breath is filling this chakra, and mentally saying "Ram, Ram, Ram, Ram." As you breathe in and intone "Ram," visualize and feel this area being filled with a bright yellow energy. Retain your breath for sixteen counts, mentally saying "Ram" with each count, visualizing and feeling the energy brightening and vibrating. Exhale, verbally saying "Ram" for eight counts. Repeat this process four times.

6. Move your attention to your heart, or *anahata*, chakra. Open this area with imaginary hands. Exhale completely, then slowly fill your lungs to a count of four, imagining that the breath is filling this chakra, and mentally saying "Yam, Yam, Yam, Yam." As you breathe in and intone "Yam," visualize and feel this area being filled with a bright green energy. Retain your breath for sixteen counts, mentally saying "Yam" with each count, visualizing and feeling the energy brightening and vibrating. Exhale, verbally saying "Yam" for eight counts. Repeat this process four times.

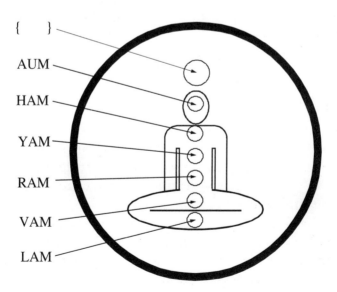

Figure 36. The seed sounds of the seven chakras.

7. Move your attention to your throat, or *vishuddha*, chakra. Open this area with imaginary hands. Exhale completely, then slowly fill your lungs to a count of four, imagining that the breath is filling this chakra, and mentally saying "Ham, Ham, Ham, Ham." As you breathe in and intone "Ham," visualize and feel this area being filled with a bright blue energy. Retain your breath for sixteen counts, mentally saying "Ham" with each count, visualizing and feeling the energy brightening and vibrating. Exhale, verbally saying "Ham" for eight counts. Repeat this process four times.

8. Move your attention to your third eye, or *ajna*, chakra. Open this area with imaginary hands. Exhale completely, then slowly fill your lungs to a count of four, imagining that the breath is filling this chakra, and mentally saying "Aum, Aum, Aum, Aum." As you breathe in and intone "Aum," visualize and feel this area filled with a bright indigo energy. Retain your breath for sixteen counts, mentally saying "Aum" with each count, visualizing and feeling the energy brightening and vibrating. Exhale, verbally saying "Aum" for eight counts. Repeat this process four times.

9. Move your attention to your crown, or *sahasrara*, chakra. Open this area with imaginary hands. Exhale completely, then slowly fill your lungs to a count of four, imagining that the breath is filling this chakra, and mentally being silent in the space between sounds. As you breathe in and intone silence, visualize and feel this area being filled with a bright violet energy. Retain your breath silently for sixteen counts, visualizing and feeling the energy brightening and vibrating. Exhale for eight counts. Repeat this process four times.

10. Now that your energy channel is open, on an inhalation, visualize and feel that cosmic energy is flowing in from above through you crown chakra and moving down into your heart chakra. As you exhale, visualize and feel that this energy is flowing through you down deep into the earth.

11. As you inhale, visualize and feel earth energy flowing up through your base chakra into your heart chakra, and as you

exhale, visualize and feel the earth energy flowing up through your crown chakra and out into the cosmos.

12. Inhale, visualizing and feeling cosmic and earth energy flowing from above and below through your chakras to your heart chakra. As you exhale, radiate this energy out in all directions, filling the universe.
13. Repeat steps 10 through 12 as many times as you like.
14. Return to normal consciousness.

Manifesting Synchronicity: New Hermetics Creative Visualization

The following is a simple tool for creating any manifestation in your life. You can use this tool for anything from improving your self-confidence to attracting new relationships or creating an influx of financial abundance. In order for this tool to work, it requires that you believe it will work. I recommend that you use this tool for simple, easily manifested results at first, and then build to larger manifestations as you begin to believe in your own power. If you use this tool without believing that it will work, this lack of belief will completely negate its effectiveness. Simply choose something that you want to occur in your life, and perform the following.

1. Enter the altered state using your meditation anchor (see page 132).
2. Go to your inner temple (see page 90).
3. Perform the New Hermetics grounding and centering (see page 99).
4. Start to visualize past times when you have experienced the desired manifestation, or some part of it, or think of someone who has experienced what you want. Fully associate with this experience, seeing the images, feeling the feelings, and hearing the sounds of this past experience, or those of the person who has experienced it.
5. Check in with yourself to make sure this is something that you really want to experience in your life. Make any necessary adjustments to your desire.

Figure 37. Visualize a movie screen in the middle of your inner temple.

6. Visualize a white screen in the middle of your inner temple, like a movie screen (see figure 37, above).
7. Now create a detailed movie of the desire up on this screen, watching yourself from the outside, experiencing your desire exactly the way that you'd like it to manifest (see figure 38, opposite).
8. Check in with yourself again, making sure that every part of your being really wants this to occur. Satisfy any objections that come up by adjusting the content of your movie.
9. Step into your movie, experiencing it in the first person, from the inside, seeing, feeling, and hearing all of the content that you would like to occur (see figure 39, opposite).
10. Step out of the movie, and look up at the globe of white light above you. Visualize a beam of power descending onto you. See and feel yourself filling with light and power until you are filled with a sense of ultimate power (see figure 40, page 148).

Figure 38. Create a detailed movie of your desire.

Figure 39. Experience your movie in the first person.

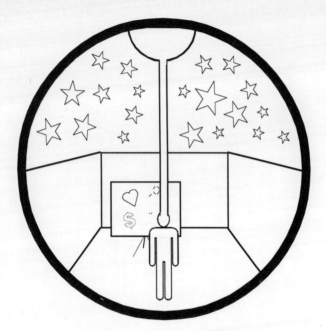

Figure 40. Imagine a beam of power descending
onto you from the globe of light.

11. Feeling this awesome power within you, look up at the globe
    again and tell your cosmic consciousness that you would like
    this desire that you have turned into a detailed movie, or
    something even better, to manifest in your life in a totally
    harmonious and beneficial way.
12. Project all of the energy that your cosmic consciousness has
    given you into the movie, feeling and seeing it flow. Visualize
    the movie starting to glow (see figure 41, opposite).
13. Visualize the movie screen floating upward and flying into
    the globe of light above you, to be manifested by the forces
    of consciousness (see figure 42, opposite).
14. Now, move your mind forward into the future, entering a
    time when you have already experienced the desire. Fully
    experience this result, visually, auditorily, and kinesthetically
15. Return to your inner temple. Perform the New Hermetics
    grounding and centering.
16. Return to normal awareness.

Figure 41. Project power into your movie.

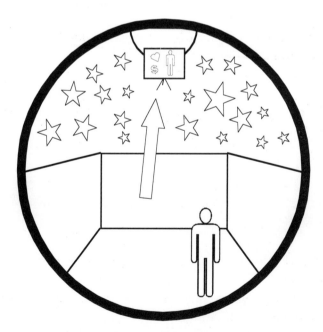

Figure 42. See the movie screen floating up into the globe of light.

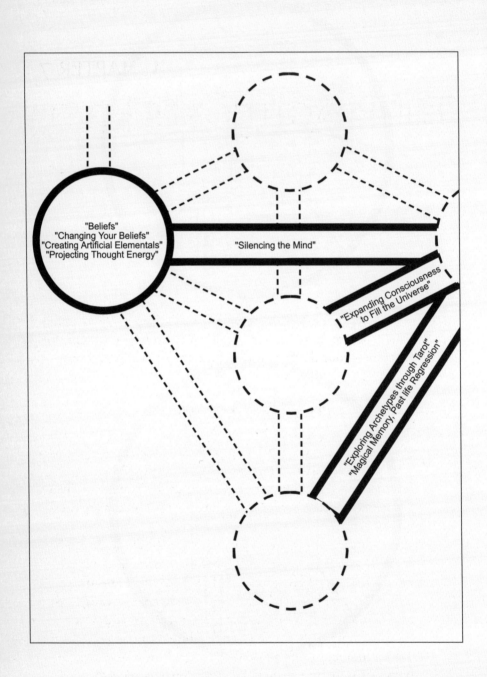

CHAPTER 7

THE PRACTITIONER LEVEL

A t this level, you will explore your mental life, begin to understand the structures of your inner world, and gain practical tools for changing your thinking process and the world around you.

THE POWER OF GOALS

Let's take another look at the goals you formulated in chapter 5, particularly the top five. Have you accomplished any of your goals yet? Are there any of your goals that you no longer want to pursue?

1. Make a new list of all your goals, and choose a new top five. It's perfectly all right if nothing has changed, just write them all out again.

2. For each of your top five goals, state specifically what you want in detail—the amounts, environment, what it will feel like in sensory terms, what it will look like, what people around you will say, right down to the detail. Get really creative and excited. Write at least a paragraph for each goal.

3. Some of your goals may be fairly ambitious and complicated. Take a moment to break down your goals into several increments or steps and write these steps down. What will the

intervening phases between now and the complete accomplishment of your goals be like? In other words, if your goal
is to become president of a large corporation, you might
break it down something like this: learn about corporate
America, get a job at a corporation, get an MBA, move into
an executive position, perform amazingly in that position,
innovate for the company, take over. You may create as many
steps or stages as you like for each goal.

4. Once you have done this, think of another small thing that
   you could do right now to begin the process of accomplishing each of these five goals. Again, it doesn't have to be a big
   thing, just write down something you can do to begin the
   process of accomplishing your top five goals.

Be sure to do these five small things. You will set in motion massive forces
in the universe. Once you have accomplished each of these small tasks,
you can do the preceding exercise with the rest of your goals, or you can
wait so you don't become psychically confused by trying to accomplish
too much. This simple exercise has changed your entire destiny.

Exploring Archetypes—Tarot Trumps

This is a general tool that can be adapted to many needs. You can use
specific tarot cards that you are interested in exploring, rather than letting fate choose for you. You can choose to explore the Major Arcana,
or trumps, in order, from 0-22 or from 22-0. You will need to work
with all of these archetypes eventually, but you may approach it from
whichever direction you prefer initially.

The purpose of this tool is to get in touch with the universal archetypal energies depicted in the trumps of the tarot deck. These cards
make up a fairly complete set of archetypes for your use. By beginning
to understand the components of these archetypes and their expectations of you, you will gain access to much greater understanding of your
own unconscious needs and desires. When you are asking these archetypes what they need from you, be sure that you really listen to the
answers you receive and think about what those answers mean. They
have the power to transform your life instantly if you listen.

Allow yourself to be open as you experience these personalities, and do not try to force them to conform to your conscious expectations. This will degrade your experience to mere fantasy, although, as I've said before, even fantasy can be transformative. Allow yourself to experience the personality of each card fully as it manifests to you. It may seem quite unlike the image depicted on the card, and this is really a sign that you are on the right track. The archetypes have a different meaning for each of us, and will manifest idiosyncratically to everyone. Some of the archetypes may seem fearsome or incredibly seductive. Think about what this means as you are experiencing the encounter and afterward. These archetypal energies have real messages that are distinctly, personally for you. It will be to your great advantage to listen carefully. Don't expect communication lines to be clear. You will receive symbols, words, feelings—in short: archetypal communication.

If you are at all confused, seek counsel from your inner teacher. Your inner teacher can help you to unfold the mysteries of symbolic communication if you allow it. Your inner teacher will always be with you as you encounter these archetypal energies, so do not be afraid to ask for assistance if things seem to get intense.

You can also adapt this tool to be used with other symbols, but the tarot really gives a fairly complete set of archetypal ideas. Table 10 (see page 154) gives a short list of some of the archetypal ideas contained in the 22 tarot trumps.

It is recommended, for the purposes of the New Hermetics, that you use the Rider-Waite, Thoth, or BOTA Tarot deck. The images in these cards represent the archetypal forces in a fairly pure and unadulterated way (with exceptions, of course). There are many other excellent decks, but for the most part, they interpret the archetypes within a milieu. For instance, without intending to step on any toes, there are decks based on Celtic or Arthurian legend, Egyptian gods, Norse gods, Voodoo loa, etc. These are particular cases of the archetypes, not the kernel or truth that is at their core. These more specific images may be very useful for divination or other types of meditation, but this tool is meant to put you in touch with the universal essence behind the various veils of mythology. However, you will do as you please in the long run, so just consider the above a little unsolicited advice.

Card	Hebrew Letter	Astrological Symbol	Archetypal Meaning
The Fool	א	🜁	divine folly, jester, joker, babe in the egg, the Green Man, spirit, chaos, mad genius, Dionysus
The Magician	ב	☿	Prometheus, trickster, wizard, inventor, artist, creative will, magic power, Hermes
The High Priestess	ג	☾	priestess, wise woman, yoni, gnosis, Isis, the hidden sanctuary, beauty
The Empress	ד	♀	mother nature, mother, manifester, love, wife, Demeter, queen, goddess, alchemical salt
The Emperor	ה	♈	all-father, conqueror, father, creator gods, husband, alchemical sulphur, warrior
The Hierophant	ו	♉	master, teacher, high priest, spiritual rules or laws, interpreter of the mysteries
The Lovers	ז	♊	twins, lovers, attraction of opposites, polarity, two halves of the brain
The Chariot	ח	♋	grail bearer, receptivity, reconciliation, transport, the ark, containment
Strength	ט	♌	lover, power, vitality, lust, domination, strength of love, sorceress, fascination
The Hermit	י	♍	loner, sage, path of initiation, pilgrim, inner knowledge, secret seed, secret light
The Wheel of Fortune	כ	♃	luck, karma, fate, gambler, cycles, wealth and lack, chance, expansion, success
Justice	ל	♎	balance, karma's action, balance of opposites, judge, adjustment, equilibrium, mediator, truth
The Hanged Man	מ	🜄	sacrifice, illumination, crucifixion, masochist, victim, martyr, beneficence, dissolution
Death	נ	♏	sex, angel of death, transformation, snake, scorpion, eagle, reincarnation, reproduction, completion
Temperance	ס	♐	alchemy, teacher, guide, art, guardian angel, Great Work, transformer, philosopher
The Devil	ע	♑	Pan, matter, material force, world father, Baphomet, demiurge, Satan, oppressor, redeemer
The Tower	פ	♂	nature's power, tower of Babel, dark night of the soul, phallic energy, catastrophe, eye of Shiva
The Star	צ	♒	meditation, revelation, nature's beauty, imagination, scientist, freedom, unfolding of creation
The Moon	ק	♓	illusions, dreams, night, subconscious, unconscious, fantasy, mystic, trance, right-brain
The Sun	ר	☉	self, ego, day, animus, extrovert, youth, child, aesthete, performer, left-brain, solar powers, energy
The Last Judgment	ש	🜂, ⊛	resurrection, eternal life, apocalypse, Hades, ecstasy, release
The World	ת	🜃, ♄	anima mundi, dancer, aethyr, astral light, four elements, material world, universe

Table 10. Archetypal meanings of the tarot trumps.

1. Obtain a pack of tarot cards. Separate out the 22 Major Arcana or trumps. Shuffle these trump cards so that you can choose one at random.

2. Pull one of the trump cards out of your deck. Do not look at it. Instead, put it in front of you, face down. This is an archetype that has chosen to work with you, and you must first prepare yourself.

3. Close your eyes and take several complete yogic breaths to slow down your heart rate and relax your physiology. Use your meditation anchor to enter the altered state (see page 132). It does not have to be a deep state, merely relaxed and focused. Open your eyes, remaining relaxed.

4. Turn your tarot card over and look at it. This archetypal teacher has chosen you today.

5. Become aware of the feelings that this tarot card produces in you today. What is the emotional feeling of this card? Does it seem joyful? Sad? Angry? Aloof? Mysterious? Dull? This card has some unique feeling for you, and only you can know what it is.

6. Focus your vision on the central figure of this card, whichever figure jumps out at you. Notice any symbols or tools that are present in the image.

7. Focus on the background of the card. Notice its environment and landscape. Imagine what it would be like if this were a real place. Visualize the landscape as a three-dimensional space. What sorts of sounds might you hear? Allow the environment to come alive.

8. Put the card down, and re-use your meditation anchor to move further into the altered state.

9. Go to your inner temple. Perform the New Hermetics grounding and centering (see pages 90 and 99).

10. Look to the center of your temple, and see the tarot card before you, enlarging to the size of doorway. Visualize the card opening up into a doorway, and pass through this doorway into the landscape of the card.

11. Look around this landscape until you find the central figure of the card. It will appear quickly, but it may look quite

different from the drawing on your card. This is your archetype. Ask this figure to communicate with you. When it
agrees, ask it to tell you how you can get along with it most
beneficially. Ask if it has any advice for you. Ask if it will
help you to accomplish your goals, and work with you in the
transformation of your life.

12. If the figure seems reluctant, hostile, or aggressive, ask it how
you can relate more positively with it. Consider any advice
you receive, however strange it may appear, and thank the
figure. You may ask for advice or assistance from your inner
teacher at any time in relating with the archetype.

13. When you feel that the conversation is over, say goodbye and
return from the landscape of the card to your inner temple.
Shrink the card back down to a normal size and pick it up.
Imagine that you have the rest of the cards in your other
hand, and slip the cards back into the deck.

14. Perform the New Hermetics grounding and centering and
return to normal consciousness.

15. Consider the information that the tarot archetype gave you
and take any actions that you feel appropriate as a result. Do
not ignore the advice of the archetype. You may take the
advice or not, but make that choice consciously.

ACCESSING YOUR MAGICAL MEMORY: PAST-LIFE REGRESSION

The purpose of this tool is to allow you to see the universal themes that
have brought you to where you currently are in life. With repeated use
of this tool, you may come to understand large-scale patterns that you
have been playing out over many lifetimes.

This tool does not require you to believe in literal past lives. You may
consider past lives to be metaphorical utterances from your unconscious.
It is just as helpful if you consider these past-life journeys as archetypal
stories that will explain symbolically who you really are, your challenges,
your strengths, and the lessons you are learning. With the use of this
tool, this is exactly what you will discover.

You may also view these past-life journeys as real lifetimes that you've experienced in the process of your evolution. Either way, you will learn a great deal.

1. Enter the altered state using your meditation anchor (see page 132).
2. Go to your inner temple (see page 90).
3. Perform the New Hermetics grounding and centering (see page 99).
4. Begin the process of moving back in time by visualizing a movie screen in the center of your inner temple. Recall some pleasant simple event that happened yesterday, and project it on the screen. Move into the screen and fully associate with this memory—visually, auditorily, and kinesthetically. See what you were wearing, feel your surroundings and emotions, and hear the people and sounds of yesterday.
5. Remaining fully associated, move back to a week or so ago, recalling vividly some pleasant event.
6. Remaining fully associated, move back to a month or so ago, recalling vividly some pleasant event.
7. Regress several months.
8. Go back to your early teens, remaining fully associated—visually, auditorily, and kinesthetically.
9. Regress to the age of nine or ten.
10. Regress to the age of five or six. Remain fully associated, allowing all of your senses to move back to this time.
11. Regress to age four, then age three, then age two, then age one.
12. Return to that warm, safe, secure dark place where you feel loved and surrounded by warmth and formation.
13. Try going back even further, visualizing a blue mist all around you, and feel the comfort and peace of the blue mist. It should feel very good and relaxing, and you will like it here, but you will move on, deeper into the past, visualizing a light. As you pass into this light, look down at your feet.
14. Notice what you see or feel. Look at your body. See if you're wearing shoes or clothing of any kind. Look around and see where you are. Look for other people, places, vehicles, etc.

Can you hear someone speaking to you? Do you hear a name? Is it your name from this time? What is the name of the place where you are?

15. Move to an important event that took place in this life, something that you need to learn about. Experience what this life was about. Move to other events.

16. Now move to the end of this life, and peacefully experience the death process. Begin to assimilate the message of this experience.

17. Ask yourself, what was the reason or purpose of this life? What were the lessons? What did you leave incomplete? What were your joys?

18. Look into the eyes of yourself in this life, and into the eyes of those you loved, and send your love to these beings, saying goodbye and allowing them to fade.

19. Allow yourself to be surrounded again by light, and travel through this light to the blue mist. Emerge from the blue mist back to present time, returning to your inner temple.

20. Perform the New Hermetics grounding and centering.

21. Return to normal consciousness and consider deeply what you have learned.

BELIEFS OF THE NEW HERMETICS MASTERS

We have not consciously chosen our beliefs, and yet they rule our lives. We are completely limited by the beliefs that we hold about ourselves, our lives, and the world around us. And yet, these beliefs are not reality. They are structures or limitations that we place upon reality. They are the rules by which we operate, but they do not reflect reality. They merely reflect the conditioning of our environments. We do not choose our beliefs; they are implanted in us by our family, friends, jobs, etc. What's more, we often possess conflicting beliefs that stop us from accomplishing our desires. But we can consciously choose to alter our beliefs and thus enrich our lives.

Some of the empowering beliefs of the Masters of the New Hermetics are shown below.

The universe is ultimately one thing.

The universe is an expression of intelligence.

Polarity is the expression of one thing at two extreme degrees of perception.

Triplicity is one thing expressing itself in a cycle, such as a perceiver, a perceived, and the process of perception.

It is only possible to imprison yourself. Freedom is the birthright of everything.

In life, you are constantly learning, growing, and evolving.

You only need your own approval. As long as you are living up to your own expectations, you are living correctly.

When given complete information, all people attempt to do the right thing.

You are the source of all that you need.

Everything always turns out right.

The universe is infinitely abundant. The possibilities are unlimited.

In the province of the mind, what is believed to be true is true, or becomes true within certain limits, to be learned by experience and experiment. In the province of the mind, there are no limits.

The universe functions according to rules, although, at any given time, some of these rules may not be understood.

You are always connected to the source of your own strength, intelligence, creativity, and joy.

There is a subtle realm beyond matter, from which the physical universe manifests.

Everything that you need to know is within you.

It is possible to make your own luck and synchronicities, and thereby shape your own destiny.

You can often accomplish more by doing less.

If you remember to look, you discover that good things are happening to you all the time.

You are a loving being.

You are a cause for the world as you experience it.

You can change your emotional state and feel good whenever you choose.

People are basically good.

All things are ultimately eternal, having their real existence out-
　　side of the world of perceptions.
You are a necessary part of the universe.
Love is all you need.

With the next tool, you will specifically use a technology to change your
beliefs, but with this exercise, you are merely asked to consider these
wise beliefs and whether they are something that you may want to incorporate into your life.

1.　Look over each belief individually and ask yourself the fol-
　　lowing questions. Write the belief and your answers down so
　　that you may begin to gain some understanding of the pat-
　　terns that have created your beliefs and your doubts.

　　• What do I think of this belief?
　　• Is this something that I believe?
　　• Would I like to believe this?
　　• What doubts do I have about this belief?
　　• Where do these doubts originate? From friends? Family?
　　　Role models?
　　• Are these people that I really want to have this sort of influ-
　　　ence over me?
　　• Are they people that I really want to emulate?

2.　Write down some of your beliefs. What are the rules by
　　which you live? To find out some of your rules, ask yourself
　　the following questions.

　　• What do I think of myself?
　　• Who am I?
　　• What do I expect in a relationship?
　　• What does it mean to be a friend?
　　• What do I expect in a job?
　　• What is my definition of success?
　　• What is my definition of failure?
　　• How do I define God?

- How do I know when someone respects me?
- How do I know when someone cares about me?
- How do I know when somebody dislikes me?
- What is the world like?
- What are people like?

By answering these questions honestly, you will begin to understand some of your beliefs about life. You can ask yourself the same sorts of questions about any aspects of your life, and you will discover all of the beliefs and rules that construct your reality. In fact, you probably will do this. But for now, simply answer the above questions. As you come to desire a deeper knowledge of yourself, you will ask more questions and get more answers.

Now, you must understand that these are your beliefs, and do not represent facts. They are simply ideas. Many people confuse their beliefs, with reality. They think that everyone operates from the same beliefs or they believe that those who don't share their beliefs are crazy, inferior, or morally objectionable. This couldn't be further from the truth.

These beliefs that you are beginning to discover are simply cultural and familial implants into your consciousness. Some people think that their beliefs are original, that they've created them themselves. These people are just deluding themselves. Even if you disagree with what everyone has told you all your life, your beliefs were formed as rebellion against others, not created in a vacuum.

Ask yourself the following questions about the beliefs you have formulated to discover your feelings and the source of these beliefs. Some of the sources for your beliefs will be obvious. You'll say, "Oh! My mother used to say that all the time." Others will be subtler, and you'll really have to think about them.

- What do I think of this belief?
- Is this something that I really believe?
- Do I want to believe this?

- What doubts do I have about this belief?
- Where does this belief originate? From friends? Family? Role models? Rebelling against these?
- Are these people that I really want to have this sort of influence over me?
- Are they people that I really want to emulate or rebel against?

3. Write down some negative or limiting beliefs that you currently have about yourself. With the next tool, you will learn a technology for changing your limiting beliefs into empowering ones, as well as implanting positive new beliefs such as those of the New Hermetics masters.

CHANGING YOUR BELIEFS

This tool can be used to rid yourself of a negative belief or to install a positive new one, such as those of the New Hermetics Masters (see above). To use this tool with a negative belief, identify the negative belief, and then think of a positive belief to replace it. In other words, if your belief is currently, "I'm stupid," replace it with something like, "I am intelligent in many ways, and I'm becoming more and more intelligent every day." Be sure to make your new belief as positive as possible. Really make sure that the new belief is stated in extremely positive terms, without negations such as "not" or "won't." "I'm not that stupid," is not an appropriate replacement belief.

If you are using this tool to install a new positive belief, rather than just replacing a negative one, identify your current belief about the subject. This belief will be somewhat less positive than the one you'd like to install, or you will really just be wasting your time.

In order to use this tool most effectively, you must first identify the submodalities that drive belief for you. These are particular qualities of seeing, hearing, or feeling. To do this, follow the simple procedure below.

1. Think about the negative belief that you currently have. As you think about it, are you making pictures, hearing sounds, experiencing feelings? Where are these experiences in your mind or body? What are the qualities of these experiences?

Big? Bright? Dull? Loud? Intense? Make a list, mentally or on paper, of the specific submodalities. These are your belief submodalities.

2. Think about something that you doubt—something such as, "The world may be flat," or "Dirt could taste good." Make sure it doesn't have any serious emotional content, so you can just experience the statement for what it is. As you think about this, are you making pictures, hearings sounds, or experiencing feelings? Where are these experiences in your mind or body? What are the qualities of these experiences? Big? Bright? Dull? Loud? Intense? Make a list, mentally or on paper, of the specific submodalities. These are your doubt submodalities.

3. Now compare and contrast these two lists of submodalities to discover where they differ.

4. Experiment with adjusting these submodalities to discover which ones change your experience of the belief the most. Once you have figured out the submodality that has the greatest effect, you are ready to proceed. Simply use this submodality as the changing factor in the tool below. You can change more than one submodality if you feel it will be helpful.

Belief Change

Once you have identified your belief and doubt submodalities, follow these simple steps to change a belief.

1. Enter the altered state using your meditation anchor (see page 132).

2. Go to your inner temple (see page 90).

3. Perform the New Hermetics grounding and centering (see page 99).

4. Move to the front or east of your inner temple. You will be right in front of the yellow wall, the air quadrant of the temple. As you visualize this yellow wall, see a clear sky, feel the blowing of a pleasant breeze. Just like the ever-changing

wind, your thoughts shift and change constantly. You can
change them effortlessly.

5. Identify your negative belief. Feel the weight of this belief
    on your life and how it is negatively impacting your life right
    now.

6. Step out into the air quadrant, and allow yourself to move
    forward into the future five years. See, hear, and feel how
    your life will be if you hold onto this negative belief.
    Imagine all of the worst possible things that could happen to
    you. Feel all the pain that this belief will cause you, holding
    onto it for five more years. What will you miss? Relationships?
    Experiences? Opportunities? Really *feel* the pain.

7. Allow yourself to move forward into the future fifteen years.
    See, hear, and feel how much worse your life will be if you
    hold onto this negative belief. Imagine all of the worst pos-
    sible things that could happen to you. Feel all the pain that
    this belief will cause you, holding onto it for fifteen more
    years. What will you miss? Relationships? Experiences?
    Opportunities? Really *feel* all of that pain.

8. Return to your inner temple, and again face the east.

9. As you think about your negative belief, keeping the con-
    tent the same, adjust the submodalities of this belief that
    you discovered before. Change the submodalities to your
    doubt submodalities.

10. Switch the submodalities back and forth several times from
    your belief submodalities to your doubt submodalities. Stop
    with the negative belief in your doubt submodalities. Now
    turn down all of your representations, until the negative
    belief is no longer present.

11. Think of the positive belief that you are putting in place of
    the negative one. Put it into your belief submodalities.
    Switch the submodalities back and forth several times from
    your belief submodalities to your doubt submodalities. Stop
    with the positive belief in your belief submodalities.

12. Amplify all of your representations of this new belief, so that it
    is the most intensely positive experience you can have. Make it
    really compelling and exciting. Experience it as a reality.

13. Move out into the air quadrant, and move forward to tomorrow. Experience your consciousness with this new belief. Experience the positive changes as you move through your day.

14. Move forward into the future five years. Experience all of the benefits that have entered your life as a result of this new belief. Experience all of the joys, experiences, and opportunities that have opened up for you with this new belief in your life for five years.

15. Move forward fifteen years. Experience all of the wonderful things in your life due to this new belief. Really experience the joy of this belief in your life.

16. Return to your inner temple.

17. Perform the New Hermetics grounding and centering.

18. Return to normal consciousness, and test yourself to make sure that you have really changed your belief. If it is not completely changed, repeat the pattern, adjusting submodalities as needed.

PROJECTION OF ENERGY TO CHARGE SPACES

This tool is used to charge a room, or house, or any space with a desired energy. You may use this tool to charge your house with vital energy, giving you a boost of energy every time you enter. You can charge your bedroom with relaxing energy to help you drift off to sleep at night. You can even charge your car with negative energy when parking in the city to keep away thieves. You can also use this tool with elemental energy (fire, water, air, earth) or planetary energy.

You may want to charge your study with air energy to assist you in intellectual matters or fire energy for creativity or passion. You may want to charge your bedroom with the energy of Venus to create an amorous atmosphere. Elemental and planetary charging will become especially useful later on when you are working with specific gods or spirits.

If you are using elemental energies, you may want to face the appropriate quadrant of your inner temple. For all other energies, you may direct yourself in any way. It may be useful for you to imagine specific colors to assist you in drawing the appropriate energy into your environment. For general types of energy such as vital power, creativity, peace, joy, bliss, excitement, or relaxation, you may simply imagine a white or blue-white light. Table 11 (opposite) recommends specific elements or planets and colors for specific magical energies. You may of course use any color that you feel is most appropriate in any case.

You can use the information in Table 11 as a leaping-off point for getting really creative. You can also charge spaces with more generalized "white-light" energy for any of the above purposes. Don't feel restricted by the elemental and planetary energies. A lot of people find them very effective, however, because they have been used this way for centuries and have a lot of built-in power.

You may also charge spaces at a distance. For instance, if you have an important business meeting, you can draw in vital power or earth energy and impress upon it a desire to have a successful meeting. You can then send this energy to the room where your meeting will take place. Your meeting will go amazingly well. Use your imagination and really use this tool to enhance your world. As with all of the magical tools of the New Hermetics, it is important to believe that this will work. You should start with small things at first and build up to greater ones.

While you are drawing the energy that you desire, you must make a couple of decisions and impress them upon the energy you're accumulating. First, you must decide what specific purpose this energy will serve. Second, you must decide how long it will remain where you are sending it. You may charge a space for five minutes, five days, five years, perpetually, or any amount of time in between. You must simply decide and project that choice with the energy.

1. Enter the altered state using your meditation anchor (see page 132).
2. Go to your inner temple (see page 90).
3. Perform the New Hermetics grounding and centering (see page 99).
4. Visualize the desired energy (vital power, ecstasy, Jupiter, etc.) as filling the entire universe in a diluted, but all encompassing, form (see figure 43, page 168). In this diluted form, it is mixed with all other energies. However, become aware of this particular energy by imagining an appropriate color, sound, or feeling.

Element/ Planet	Color	Purpose
Fire	red or red-orange	success, passion, sex, lust, creativity, intuition, strength, will
Water	blue or blue-green	friendship, love, tranquility, healing, emotions, rest, understanding
Air	yellow or blue	education, memory, intellect, teaching, communication, travel, writing, theories, organizing
Earth	green, black, or brown	money, jobs, promotions, investments, health, business, physical body, construction, physical appearance
Saturn	black or violet	structures, limitation, responsibility, seriousness, reincarnation, death, inheritances, old age
Jupiter	blue or violet	generosity, abundance, leadership, vision, acquiring wealth, legal issues, luck, expansion
Mars	red	justice, strength, force, violence, energy, war, aggression, courage, competition, athletics, masculinity
Sun	yellow or gold	harmony, balance, wholeness, health, regain youth, peace, illumination, obtaining money, divine power
Venus	green	love, desire, aesthetics, nurture, beauty, pleasure, art, luxury, aphrodisiac, perfume, femininity
Mercury	orange or mixed colors	reason, communication, logic, knowledge, travel, writing, school, science, medicine, mathematics, the mind
Moon	violet, blue, or silver	imagination, instinct, subconscious, emotion, the astral world, clairvoyance, dreams, sleep, the sea

Table 11. Elements, planets, and colors for magical purposes.

5. Begin pore breathing (see page 98), drawing the appropriate energy into your body through all of your pores. Fill yourself with this energy until you feel you could nearly burst (see figure 44, page 169). Experience this energy palpably, visibly, inside your body, both in your inner temple and in your physical body.

6. Express to this energy THE specific purpose it will serve and how long it will remain in effect.

7. Allow the energy to move out of your solar plexus to fill the space you have chosen to charge. Visualize the energy filling the space you are charging (see figure 45, page 170). It is ideal for you to actually be in this room, but not absolutely necessary.

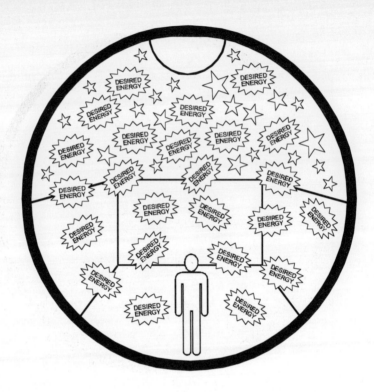

Figure 43. Imagine the desired energy filling the universe in diluted form.

8.   Repeat this process until you experience that the space is fully charged. You will know when you have succeeded by how you feel.
9.   Perform the New Hermetics grounding and centering.
10. Return to normal awareness.

CREATING ARTIFICIAL ELEMENTALS

Artificial elementals are projected thought forms that possess a certain sentience and ability to act on their own to accomplish your desires. You can create elementals to accomplish all sorts of tasks, from bringing you business contacts or lovers to manifesting wealth. You can create elementals to help you accomplish any of your goals. If you are an overeater, you can create an elemental to keep you away from the refrigerator. If you need some extra cash, you can create an elemental to man-

Figure 44. Begin pore breathing.

ifest money into your life. Anything is possible. As with all of these tools, start with small things first, until you perfect the technique.

When creating an elemental you must decide four things:

- The specific purpose that your elemental will serve.
- The name of your elemental. The name can be anything you choose, but it may be appropriate to choose a name that has something to do with its purpose.
- The amount of time it has to accomplish its mission.
- The specific date and time when it will disintegrate. You should always create an end-time for your artificial elementals, or they will continue to hang around and perhaps cause problems. For instance, if you created an elemental to bring you a relationship and the elemental stayed around, what

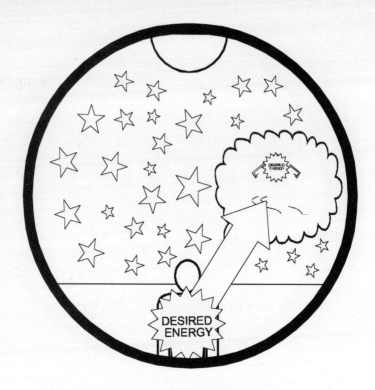

Figure 45. Imagine the desired energy moving
out of your solar plexus and filling the space you have chosen.

would become of it if the relationship ended? It might cause
some sort of complex or obsession.

You can create an elemental to perform a task over a long period of time,
but you should always have an end-time. This can be the day that you
die, if you choose. If you have a long-term elemental, you may wish to
recharge it from time to time. Simply follow the procedure below, first
calling back your elemental to get recharged. For long-term elementals,
you may want to have a physical object such as a statue, figurine, or picture as its home base. This will give you a reference point for working
with it over time.

As far as colors and specific purposes go, you may follow the advice
in the projecting energy tool above.

1. Enter the altered state using your meditation anchor (see page 132).
2. Go to your inner temple (see page 90).
3. Perform the New Hermetics grounding and centering (see page 99).
4. Visualize the desired energy (vital power, ecstasy, Jupiter, etc.) as filling the entire universe in a diluted, but all encompassing, form. In this diluted form, it is mixed with all other energies. However, become aware of this particular energy by imagining an appropriate color, sound, feeling.
5. Imagine the energy (visualizing appropriate colors, feelings, etc.) beginning to accumulate as you concentrate on it.
6. Begin pore breathing (see page 98), drawing the appropriate energy into your body through all of your pores. Fill yourself with this energy until you feel you could nearly burst. Experience this energy palpably, visibly, inside your body, both in your inner temple and in your physical body.
7. Hold out your hands in front of you, both in your inner temple and the physical world.
8. Allow the energy to move out of your solar plexus to form a sphere between ten and twenty inches between your two hands (see figure 46, page 172). Make sure that this visualization is as vivid as possible in appropriate color and intensity (turn up the brightness submodality).
9. Once you have gathered a sufficient amount of energy into this sphere, tell the elemental its name, its purpose, how long it has to accomplish it, and when it will disintegrate back into the aethyr.
10. Visualize the elemental moving up into the white globe above your inner temple to accomplish its task (see figure 47, page 173).
11. Perform the New Hermetics grounding and centering.
12. Return to normal consciousness and forget entirely about this elemental, letting it do its job without your mental, emotional, or physical interference, except where necessary. For instance, if you made an elemental to find you a job, it would be foolish not to look in the help-wanted section.

You may want to write down the conditions you created for the elemental's existence and purpose so that you can check its success or failure at a future date without having to keep it on your mind. You should really endeavor not to think about your elementals at all unless giving them specific instructions, as this will tend to hinder their effectiveness.

EXPANDING YOUR CONSCIOUSNESS TO FILL THE UNIVERSE

This is a tool that can be used to begin to comprehend the infinity of the universe, and that your consciousness is capable of encompassing this infinity. You have already experienced this infinity to a certain extent in your initiation, as well as in your death and rebirth experience. The purpose of this tool is to get you used to the idea of an expanded identity so that you will be able to operate with greater and greater power in your life and be prepared for the cosmic consciousness experience.

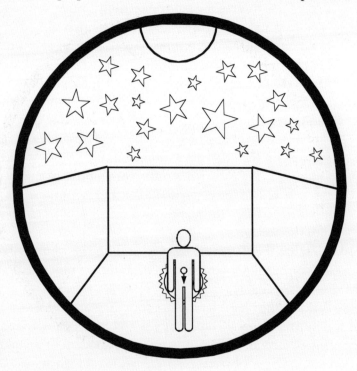

Figure 46. Imagine the desired energy moving out of your solar plexus and forming a glowing sphere.

With this tool, you will learn to expand your consciousness in a more or less intellectual way to encompass more and more of the universe. In your initiation, you basically just visualized expanded consciousness. In the Zealot phase, with the Death and Rebirth tool, you began to feel expanded consciousness emotionally. With this tool, you will come to understand expanded consciousness intellectually. Likewise, at the Philosopher level, you will expand your consciousness with your will, using the tool called Rising on the Planes.

1. Enter the altered state using your meditation anchor (see page 132).
2. Go to your inner temple (see page 90).
3. Perform the New Hermetics grounding and centering (see page 99).

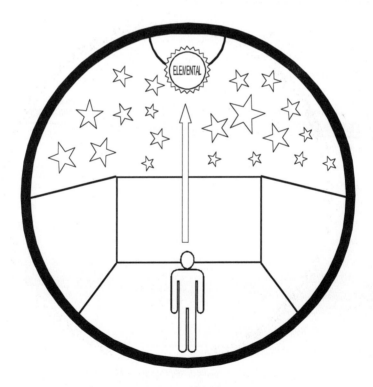

Figure 47. Visualize the elemental moving up into the globe of light above your temple.

4. Visualize the Earth, imagining particularly its size as compared with your physical body. Remember that the Earth is approximately 24,000 miles in circumference, while you are less than 0.0001 mile in circumference. Enlarge your consciousness to encompass the Earth.

5. Expand your vision to include the moon, remembering that the moon is about 180,000 miles away from the Earth.

6. Add Venus, Mars, Mercury, and the Sun to your vision.

7. You may now move your point of view to the center of the Sun.

8. Add the asteroid belt, Jupiter, Saturn, Uranus, and Pluto to your vision.

9. Expand your vision to include several solar systems.

10. Expand your vision to the entire Milky Way galaxy. Move your consciousness to the center of the galaxy.

11. Expand your vision to several galaxies.

12. Expand your vision to whole strings of galaxies.

13. Continue expanding until you conceive of the entire universe as one thing.

14. Return to your inner temple.

15. Perform the New Hermetics grounding and centering.

16. Return to normal consciousness.

SILENCING YOUR MIND

This tool is one method, the active method, of silencing thought. It is a "martial" method, requiring you to be focused and determined. It may take several attempts to master. The purpose of this tool is to teach you how the structure of your thinking process works and to provide you with a tool for making your mind silent. It is only in silence that true cosmic consciousness manifests.

1. Enter the altered state using your meditation anchor (see page 132).

2. Go to your inner temple (see page 90).

3. Perform the New Hermetics grounding and centering (see page 99).

4. Observe your thoughts passively, allowing yourself to calm and slow down.

5. As you do this, you will discover the place in your mind where your thoughts originate. Thoughts may come to you as images, words, or feelings.

6. You will become active, while remaining relaxed, identifying yourself with a desire to stop these thoughts at the point where they begin. As each new thought comes into your mind, cause images to explode, disintegrate, or fade. Turn voices down until they're inaudible. Jettison feelings out of your body. You will find finer and finer layers of thought as you go.

7. Once you are able to destroy each thought as it occurs, destroy your thoughts even as they are beginning to form. Destroy the beginnings of thought.

8. Finally, destroy the ultimate cause of thoughts, the thinker. Do this by simply shutting down all of your representational systems. You will be in pure silence. This is sometimes called the opening of the eye of Shiva—the destruction of the universe.

9. After a time, return to your inner temple.

10. Perform the New Hermetics grounding and centering.

11. Return to normal consciousness.

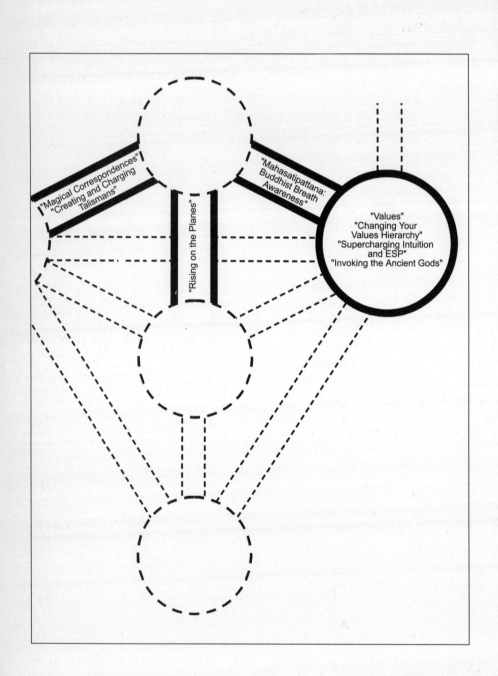

CHAPTER 8

THE PHILOSOPHER LEVEL

A t this level, you will explore your values and your intuition and begin to comprehend the totality of your inner world. You will learn how to create an intimate connection with the collective unconscious through the archetypes of the ancient gods and learn the principles of practical talismanic magick.

MAGICK, MYSTICISM, AND MAGNETISM

Magnetism is the irresistible attraction of one object toward another via an electrical or invisible field. In traditional science, this class of phenomena is usually restricted to material objects. However, this phenomenon is universal when applied to the realm beyond the physical. The human mind is irresistibly attracted to one idea or another, and ideas or spirits may be attracted into the mind of any human if you know the proper method. Take, for instance, the cheap sort of a person. Simply implying that something can be gotten for *free* is enough to attract this type of person to any sort of product or service. In fact, the whole field of advertising is based upon the manipulation of a subtle, psychic magnetism.

Words and pictures have always had an immense spiritual power. It is, after all, because of these things that we consider ourselves above the level of animal intelligence. Our ability to separate a thing quite ordinary and inert into an abstract idea of power and beauty is the source of all of the philosophy, art, and science of mankind. The gods are simply the most sublime icons of our own abstract thinking.

The most simple and direct method of magnetically attracting an idea into our lives is by constructing a precise summary of the desire for our minds. A talisman is a perfect example of this. Talismans have the advantage of convenience over many other forms of magick because, as physical objects, they tend to work even in the case of a totally incompetent magician. The only thing left to you, the magician, is to construct a talisman that accurately reflects your desire and to create an atmosphere wherein it can be "charged" by the invisible force you seek.

This section does not present an actual tool per se, but rather a set of tools that will enable you to connect with the planetary energies for the purpose of creating talismans. These archetypal energies form the basis of most sophisticated forms of magick, as well as a system for understanding your unconscious drives and repressions. Table 12 (below) reviews the basic correspondences of the planetary energies. You should also review the Projection of Energy tool in chapter 7 for more information about these energies.

To get in touch with these energies most effectively, there are a number of congruent colors, shapes, and odors that help your mind connect to the specific powers associated with each of them. The idea is that, on an unconscious level, our minds connect automatically with these energies when they are placed in proximity to congruent objects, ideas, or sensations. By using these correspondences, you quickly connect with the

Planet	Correspondence
Saturn	Structure, limitation, seriousness, responsibility
Jupiter	Generosity, abundance, leadership, vision
Mars	Justice, strength, force, violence
Sun	Beauty, harmony, balance, wholeness
Venus	Love, passion, aesthetics, nurture
Mercury	Reason, communication, logic, knowledge
Moon	Imagination, instinct, subconscious, emotion

Table 12. Planet/energy correspondences.

No.	Planet/ Element	Color	Shape	Odor
3	Saturn	Black	Triangle	Myrrh
4	Jupiter	Blue	Square	Cedar
5	Mars	Red	Pentagram	Pepper
6	Sun	Yellow	Hexagram	Frankincense
7	Venus	Green	Septagram	Benzoin
8	Mercury	Orange	Octagram	Sandalwood
9	Moon	Violet	Enneagram	Camphor
	Fire	Red		Cinnamon
	Water	Blue		Cedar
	Air	Yellow		Sandalwood
	Earth	Black		Myrrh

Table 13. Correspondences of the Hermetic Qabala.

desired forces in your life. Table 13 (above) gives some of the associations of the Hermetic Qabala. You may, of course, discover that other associations are more personally meaningful for you, but this is a place to start.

THE SHAPES OF MAGICK
Geometrical shapes take on a special meaning in the New Hermetics because of their associations with number and form. Below are summaries of the associations of a number of shapes that contribute to the power of magick.

The Triangle
The triangle is the first solid shape. It is the first possible linear shape, and is appropriately associated with the sephirah Binah and the planet

Saturn. Medieval sorcerers used triangles to bind spirits, because they believed the limiting force of the triangle would confine the spirit. The triangle may be used in any effort to restrict, structure, or limit anything. The number three also indicates cycles and, therefore, time, also a limiting factor appropriate to Saturn. Talismans having to do with the energies of Saturn should be triangular in shape.

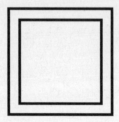

The Square

The square is related to Chesed, whose number is four. Any talisman having to do with the energies of Jupiter should be square in shape. The shape of a square implies the form of a castle or walled structure, which somewhat explains its association with society, prestige, rulership, and other Jupiterean qualities. The square also symbolizes a sort of structure that is beyond simple walls; it represents a sort of completion or perfection. We all want a "square deal" and three "square meals" a day. This shape also implies the four elements working in balanced harmony.

The Pentagram

The pentagram is the force of Mars and the sephira Geburah. The shape of the pentagram implies the human form. This corresponds to the strength of the human spirit over the four elements. We also have five fingers on each hand, the tools we use to manifest our wills in the universe. The structure of the pentagram also contains the geometry of "phi," the so-called golden mean, which indicates infinite self-replication and the golden spiral of ever-increasing expansion. Martial talismans should be five-sided.

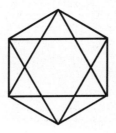

The Hexagram

The hexagram is made up of two triangles, one pointing toward the heavens, one toward earth. The number six is the number of Tiphareth, the connecting point between humanity's animal and divine natures. The number six represents balance, a perfect equilibrium between forces. Solar talismans are six-sided.

The Septagram

The number seven is associated with the days of the week, the seven ancient planets, the seven colors of the rainbow, the seven seas, and a number of other natural phenomena. It has always been considered a beneficial or "lucky" number. Seven is a number that has always had a mystical, mythical quality associated with it. Talismans associated with Venus should be seven-sided.

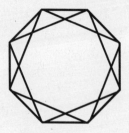

The Octagram

Eight is a number associated with systems. The octave of musical notes, the eight Chinese trigrams, and Leary's model of consciousness are a few examples. This number implies science, patterns, and knowledge of all sorts. Talismans of Mercury should be eight-sided.

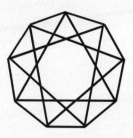

The Enneagram

Nine is the number of the Moon and the sephirah Yesod. The number nine has long been associated with the emotions. The nine muses of ancient Greece are perhaps the most obvious example. Lunar talismans should be nine-sided.

CREATING SIGILS AND TALISMANS

The easiest way to construct a talisman is to make a simple sigil or seal to represent your desire. With this tool, you can make a talisman to accomplish anything you can imagine.

1. Decide what sort of energy you are interested in attracting to your talisman. At this point, you need to decide if you are going to use one of the planetary shapes and colors for your talisman or make it round or some other shape. You must then obtain the correct materials for your talisman.

2. Take a piece of paper and first create a sentence that expresses what you want. It can be a simple sentence, but make sure that you understand what you are wanting specifically. Avoid being overly vague, because the universe may misunderstand and give you something different than what you want. An example of a decent sentence is . . .

> *It is my will that my mother's bursitis be*
> *healed in the next two weeks.*

3. On this same piece of paper, take this sentence and remove all of the repeating letters so that only one of each letter remains. For the above example it would look like this . . .

ITSMYWLHAOERBUDNXK

This then is your "word of power." It is a "barbarous word," meaningless to the conscious mind, but representative of your desire to your subconscious mind and the collective unconscious.

4. Below this, on the same piece of paper, create the sigil from these letters. Combine the letters into a shape that is pleasing to your eye. You may simplify things by including simple letters such as I or U within the shapes of other letters or representing M and considering W and V to be represented by this shape as well. You may stylize or distort letters in any way that pleases your sense of aesthetics. Figure 48 shows one way to sigilize these letters (see page 184).

5. Once you have settled on a sigil that looks right to you, draw that sigil at the center of your talisman. You should draw it in a complementary color to the color of your talisman. In other words . . .

Figure 48. Sigilized letters.

White with Black
Blue with Orange
Red with Green
Yellow with Purple

Since the above sigil is a healing sigil, I might put it into an octagram (see figure 49, opposite).

6. Once you have created your talisman you are ready to move on to the next tool to charge the talisman.

Charging Talismans

This is a simple tool for charging talismanic objects with any desire. You may use this tool for talismans created with the previous tool, or any other object that you wish to charge magically, such as a piece of jewelry or a natural object like a stone or a feather. If you are using an object other than a talisman, the object should have some relationship or correspondence with the energy with which you are charging it. In other words, if you were going to charge a stone with the energy of Mars, it is best if the stone is red, or has five sides, or something like that.

Before charging any object, you must decide three things:

* Its purpose. Why specifically are you charging it?
* Who it's for. Will the energy work just for you, for anyone who holds the object, or for someone else only?

Figure 49. A sigil placed in a magical shape.

- How long does the talisman have to accomplish its job? Two weeks? A month? Will it last forever?

The answers to these three questions form the statement of purpose that you will make in step 7 of this tool. Again, as with all of these tools, it is best to start with simple things at first and move to more complex desires as your experience and beliefs can handle them.

1. Create or obtain an object you wish to charge for some magical purpose. It is, of course, best if it is in some way associated to the desired force (i.e., if you are making a talisman of Venus to bring love, you may want to make it seven-sided or related to seven in some way, and green).
2. Sprinkle a little bit of cool fresh water on the talisman to purify it. As you are doing this, visualize that any and all energies are leaving the talisman so that it is in a totally blank slate.
3. You may wish to burn appropriate incense (see table 13, page 179).
4. Use your meditation anchor to enter the altered state (see page 132).
5. Go to your inner temple (see page 90).
6. Perform the New Hermetics grounding and centering (see page 99).

7. State the complete purpose of your talisman, at least inwardly, but preferably aloud without breaking your state. Check in with all parts of your being to make sure that this purpose is really something that you want to happen. If you experience any sensations or images of doubt or disapproval, change your statement until you feel totally congruent or else abandon this desire. Once you experience that all parts of your being congruently desire the purpose of this talisman, you can proceed.

8. Visualize the power or force you are attracting to your talisman as being outside and all around you. This may be through a combination of images, feelings, sounds, or colors. (At this point, you may also include the next tool, Invoking the Gods (see page 188) to attract the force, power, or wisdom of a specific god form. Be sure you are familiar with both tools before you use them.) You can visualize this force as descending into your inner temple or materializing from a specific quadrant, depending upon your specific needs.

9. Once you feel the definite experience of the desired force all around you (this will be a combination of visual and kinesthetic sensations), hold up your talisman, physically and in your imaginary hand in your inner temple. Visualize the force that you desire accumulating in your talisman. Accumulate all of the energy that you can into your talisman.

10. Once you have the distinct experience (again a visual and kinesthetic sense) that the desired force is permeating your talisman in as powerful a way as you are capable of accomplishing, clearly visualize your talisman, and then begin to see an image of your accomplished desire behind the image of the talisman. See this image of the accomplished desire move through your talisman until it is entirely in front of the talisman, filling your view.

11. Repeat this process of visualizing your talisman, then drawing an image of your completed desire through the image of the talisman until the imagined desire completely fills your view a number of times as quickly as possible, until the image of the

talisman automatically produces the image of your accomplished desire.
12. State the purpose of your talisman again clearly.
13. Perform the New Hermetics grounding and centering.
14. Return to normal consciousness.

Once you have charged a talisman, there are two basic things you can do with it. First, you can hold on to it or give it to the person you made it for, and the power will be available anytime you need it. This is especially appropriate for talismans that have a long-term life, or any that you feel would give better service by being physically with the person for whom you made it.

The second thing that you can do with a charged talisman is to destroy it physically, allowing it to fulfill its function astrally in the aethyr. This is, in many ways, a more elegant way of working with talismans, since you will not be left with a bunch of pieces of paper or wood lying around. It is especially useful if you will not physically be in contact with the person, place, or thing you intend to affect with your talisman. There are four basic ways of launching a talismanic force by destroying its physical vehicle. You, of course, want to use whichever one of these seems most in harmony with your purpose:

By fire. You can hold the talisman up to a candle flame or stove, or throw it into a blazing fire or on top of burning charcoal.
By water. You can put your talisman into a river or the ocean. (Be sure no one sees you so they don't disturb your talisman.) You can also make your talisman out of water-soluble ink, and then let the ink run away under the faucet or pour water onto it or place it into a dish of water.
By air. You can throw your talisman into a ravine or off a cliff. If you use water-soluble ink or paint, you can boil water and allow the steam to disintegrate the talismanic image. You can even attach your talisman to an appropriately colored helium balloon and let it go.
By earth. You can place your talisman under a rock or bury it. One very popular ancient technique was to bury a talisman under the path of the person for whom the spell was cast, so that the

energy would be released when they stepped over it. You can also make a talisman in the dirt or sand, and wipe it away once it is charged.

With any of these methods, it is important to imagine the talisman becoming free to operate in the astral plane when it is gone, rather than merely disintegrating with its physical vehicle. To accomplish this, hold onto the image of the talisman and its purpose in your mind while you are destroying it. You can then launch this astral image into the aethyr.

EXPLORING ARCHETYPES: INVOKING THE GODS

This tool can be used to connect directly with the archetypal energies of the old gods, most particularly those of the ancient Greco-Roman planetary gods. You may use this tool with any god, but please be clear about what aspects of this god may be useful for developing new abilities or personality changes in yourself. Table 14 (below) gives the Greco-Roman planetary gods with some of their qualities. This is a useful place to start.

Examine this table and choose qualities that you feel you are lacking, but that you would like to manifest in your life. You can use this tool to strengthen any area of your life or to understand aspects of these gods that you wish to explore from the inside. Use the following tool to connect with these forces and activate them in your life. Again, you may use this tool with any god you desire to know.

No.	God	Characteristics
3	Saturn/Kronos	Structures, limitation, responsibility, seriousness
4	Jupiter/Zeus	Generosity, abundance and wealth, leadership, luck
5	Mars/Ares	Strength, energy, battle, courage, competition, athletics
6	Sol/Helios/Apollo	Harmony, wholeness, peace, illumination
7	Venus/Aphrodite	Love, desire, aesthetics, beauty, pleasure, luxury
8	Mercury/Hermes	Language, logic, knowledge, science, medicine
9	Luna/Selene/Artemis	Imagination, subconscious, emotion, dreams

Table 14. Greco-Roman gods and their characteristics.

1. Enter the altered state using your meditation anchor (see page 132).
2. Go to your inner temple (see page 90).
3. Perform the New Hermetics grounding and centering (see page 99).
4. State the purpose for which you are invoking this specific god-form/energy, either aloud or at least internally directed to the area above your inner temple.
5. Begin to visualize the form of the god in front of you, hovering above your inner temple, either as an ideal human or the particular distinctive form of the god you have chosen. Visualize this form glowing intensely with an appropriately colored energy.
6. Think about the quality that you would like to gain from this god. Observe how this god is a representation of it. How is the god standing that represents your desire? What is the god seeing in its mind's eye? What is it saying to itself that fully embodies the quality that you seek in its ideal form? Ask this figure if it will communicate with you. When it agrees, ask it to tell you how you can get along with it most beneficially. Ask if it has any advice for you. Ask if it will help you to accomplish your goals, and work with you in the transformation of your life. If the figure seems reluctant, hostile, or aggressive, ask it how you can relate more positively with it. Consider any advice you receive, however strange it may appear, and thank the figure. You may ask for advice or assistance from your inner teacher at any time in relating with the archetype.
7. Stand up physically and move into the same position as the god. Imitate the way you see the god standing, the way the god is moving, etc.
8. Feel yourself and the god integrating into one form. Visualize the color of the god's force inside you. Feel the energy of this god inside you. Hear the god's voice as your own voice. See the universe the way this god sees it.
9. Make this experience even more vivid by turning up all of your submodalities.

10. Create an anchor by saying the name of the god at the peak of this experience while you are in the same position as the god. Repeat this several times to reinforce the anchor.
11. Separate from the god and thank it for sharing its being with you.
12. Sit down and reassociate yourself in your inner temple.
13. Perform the New Hermetics grounding and centering.
14. Return to normal consciousness.

You now have an anchor for establishing contact with the energy of this god in the future as well. Simply stand again in the exact position you were standing as you integrated with the god and say its name. You will again feel connected with the its power.

EXPLORING INTUITION AND ESP

The following tool is a very simple method for receiving information from the collective unconscious. It can be adapted to any purpose—finding lost articles or missing persons, finding out information about a person or event, medical intuition, or anything else that you may want to do with psychic powers or ESP. It is very similar to what ancient magick calls *skrying*. The only difference is that, with skrying, you traditionally stare into a crystal ball, black mirror, or pool of ink that is physically in front of you. With this tool, you simply create a large mirror with a flat black surface in your inner temple.

You may use this tool to ascertain information about anything you desire to know, but cannot find out by traditional means. You can also experiment with having someone else determine a question without telling you what it is. Then follow through with the tool and report your findings to the person.

You must not expect all of the information you receive to be literal. You will experience a lot of symbolic imagery, feelings, ideas, and "knowings." As you work with this tool over time, you will begin to notice repeating symbols and experiences. This is the language that the collective unconscious uses to communicate with you. Once you are able to understand the distinctions between your experiences, this tool will become incredibly valuable to you.

As always, please use this tool with simple things at first, to build your confidence in the experience and to acquaint yourself with the technology. Do not use this tool for important decisions until you are extremely experienced.

1. Enter the altered state using your meditation anchor (see page 132).
2. Go to your inner temple (see page 90).
3. Perform the New Hermetics grounding and centering (see page 99).
4. Visualize a large black mirror in the center of your inner temple. Tell yourself that this mirror is capable of showing you any information that you desire.
5. Pose a question to your mirror, or think of something you'd like to know. (You can also just look into the mirror if you do not know what you are specifically asking.)
6. You will begin to receive impressions. These may be feelings, images, or sensations. Do not try to interpret them immediately; just take note of them. Allow your intuitions to remain simple at first. Don't bother trying to determine specific things, but rather note impressions like blue, rough, soft, bright, etc. You may wish to write down your impressions on a pad of paper.
7. After a few of these more vague impressions, you may begin to receive more distinct information that relates to your inquiry. Note any of these as well.
8. Allow the black mirror to fade from view, knowing that it will be available any time you need it.
9. Perform the New Hermetics grounding and centering.
10. Return to normal consciousness.
11. Compare the information you've received to your inquiry, and attempt to make sense out of it.

VALUE HIERARCHIES

Your values are really the states that you consider the most desirable and the states that you find most detestable in your life. Values are not, at their core, desire for possessions, honors, or behavioral laws for your community, but rather the emotional states that these things may provide. For instance, comfort, security, adventure, consistency, change, wisdom, or joy are all states that may fit into your list of values. As another example, if you say you have strong family values, what you are most likely saying is that you value states like security, love, connection, and consistency, and dislike states like lust, independence, rebellion, and outrageousness.

These values really guide your life. If you value adventure, you will create a life for yourself that involves adventurous situations, even if you are not entirely conscious of it. Whereas if you value consistency or security above adventure, you will most likely avoid any overly stimulating experiences. This also affects your creativity and your will. Your values completely shape what you are willing to try, what you are willing to accomplish, even what you are willing to dream.

Like your beliefs, your values are not consciously chosen, but rather implanted by circumstance into your mind. You must now begin to examine your values and to decide whether or not your current values are consistent with who you really want to be.

Make a list of your values. Make sure these are states rather than specific quantities. As you begin to list your values, if cars or diamonds pop into your head, think about what cars or diamonds really provide for you. Opulence? Luxury? Security? Freedom? As you begin to make your lists, please be sure to be honest about how you really feel, rather than how you might prefer to feel. You will have an opportunity to adjust your lists later, but please attempt to be accurate about where you are now. It will be your eventual aim to be flexible and to make your values reflect your goals and who you really want to be. That will be later. For now, please simply try to figure out what's going on right now.

1. Create a list of your values for the following subjects in the five elemental categories:

    • Spirit—spirituality, your life's work
    • Fire—personal power, creativity, sexuality
    • Water—emotions, relationships

- Air—intellect, education, communication
- Earth—finances, physical body, work, personal environment

Ask yourself the following questions: What states do I value most in my . . . (spirituality, personal power, emotions etc.)? What states do I most want to avoid in my . . . (spirituality, personal power, emotions etc.)? Try to list several (five or more) values for each. It is okay for them to be redundant from subject to subject.

2. Think about what is most important to you, and list the top five values for each subject, both positive and negative, in order. These are your values hierarchies. Table 15 (see page 194) shows an analysis of values for the element spirit. Your lists should end up looking something like it.

3. Write down your rules for these values. What are the rules that govern these values? Ask yourself what you need to experience in order to feel that you've obtained the desired state. For instance, for love, I might say:

I experience love in my spirituality when I do something kind for someone and they don't even know it.

Establish what your rules are for all of the desired and undesired states for all of these subjects. Add these rules to the values you listed in Table 15.

4. Separately list the top five values that you feel guide your life in general.

5. Compare of these lists of values and rules with your goals and your beliefs and your emotions from previous tools. Do all of these parts of you work in harmony, or are there places where there are inconsistencies or oppositions?

Changing Your Values

You will discover as you explore the preceding tools that there are many inconsistencies between your current values and the person that you want to be as expressed in your goals. Use this tool to shift values up in

Value	Pursue	Avoid	Rule
Spirituality Life's Work	Love	Limitation	I experience love in my spirituality when I do something kind for someone and they don't even know it.
	Bliss Connection Peace Wisdom	Hatred Judgment Anger Dependence	

Table 15. Values for the element spirit.

your value hierarchy or to add new values to enhance your purposeful direction in life.

1. Enter the altered state using your meditation anchor (see page 132).
2. Go to your inner temple (see page 90).
3. Perform the New Hermetics grounding and centering (see page 99).
4. Turn to your right, to the red fire wall in your inner temple. As you look at the wall, see and feel the heat of fire. This is your fire, the driving force of your being. Move into this fire, and feel the warmth of it inside you.
5. Identify the value (specific emotional state such as joy, love, success, power, humor) that you wish to install in yourself, or move higher in your hierarchy of values.
6. Recall a specific time when you have experienced this value or state in your life or in the life of some person who you feel embodies this state. Fully immerse yourself in this specific memory until you are seeing, hearing, and feeling all of the components that you desire. Now, anchor this by saying to yourself the name of this value or state while you experience it.

7. Returning to the fiery area of your inner temple, create an imaginary scenario projected on a screen amid the flames that will take place in the future where you will experience this state as a part of your life. Create a specific scenario that, in the past, might have caused a different experience, but now will cause you to experience the desired value or state. You can make this scenario relate to your goals or to the specific element of your life to which the value relates (i.e., water—your emotional life and relationships).

8. Make sure that this change is something that you really want. Check in with all of yourself to make sure there are no feelings of doubt or hesitation. If there are objections, make adjustments to your scenario until all parts of you are satisfied.

9. Step into the movie screen and experience this scenario in the first person, seeing, hearing, and feeling as if you were really there. As you are experiencing this, again say the name of this value or state to fully anchor it.

10. Move out of the scenario, and bring the movie screen into the center of your inner temple. This movie screen is now a hologram of your desire. Send this movie screen up into the starry sky above your inner temple, asking your cosmic consciousness to place this experience into the slot in the hierarchy of values that you desire. Your cosmic consciousness will now add this value to your unconscious and express it dynamically in your life.

11. Visualize yourself tomorrow, living with this value in the place in your life you have chosen. Experience several detailed scenarios.

12. Return to your inner temple.

13. Perform the New Hermetics grounding and centering.

14. Return to normal consciousness.

15. Test this change by stating the name of the value just as you did in your inner temple and noticing whether you experience the value as a real part of you. You may use this tool several times to thoroughly install this state.

BREATH AWARENESS—MAHASATIPATHANA

This is a very simple tool, but it is quite significant in its potential impact on your consciousness. After all, it is the technique that the Buddha used to obtain his liberation. Its basic purpose is to increase and enhance your awareness of the simple process of "being." This is one example of awareness meditation. It can be expanded to awareness of thoughts and other elements of consciousness as well.

1. Enter the altered state using your meditation anchor (see page 132).
2. Observe your breath as it goes in and out.
3. Feel the sensation of the air moving through your body, cool as it enters and warm as it leaves.
4. If you become distracted, return to observing your breath when you remember. Do not be hard on yourself when distracted, simply return to your breath.
5. Try not to focus on anything else but breathing; quietly put aside thoughts, images, and feelings that come up, acknowledging them and letting them go.
6. Continue for about twenty minutes.
7. Return to normal consciousness.

RISING ON THE PLANES

This technique is again quite simple, but powerful. It is a precursor to the ultimate tool of this book, the Conscious Communion with Cosmic Consciousness. Please explore this tool a number of times before working with the Conscious Communion with Cosmic Consciousness tool.

1. Enter the altered state using your meditation anchor (see page 132).
2. Go to your inner temple (see page 90).
3. Perform the New Hermetics grounding and centering (see page 99).
4. In your astral or imaginary body, rise up out of your inner temple and travel straight upward.

5. Continue traveling straight upward without stopping for any reason. You may see or experience scenes, images, or thoughts. Ignore them and keep traveling straight up. You may feel as if there is something that stops you from going any higher. Press through this with all of your will and keep rising.
6. Continue rising until you experience either dissolution into pure light or you lose consciousness.
7. When you return to yourself, reintegrate in your inner temple.
8. Perform the New Hermetics grounding and centering.
9. Return to normal consciousness.

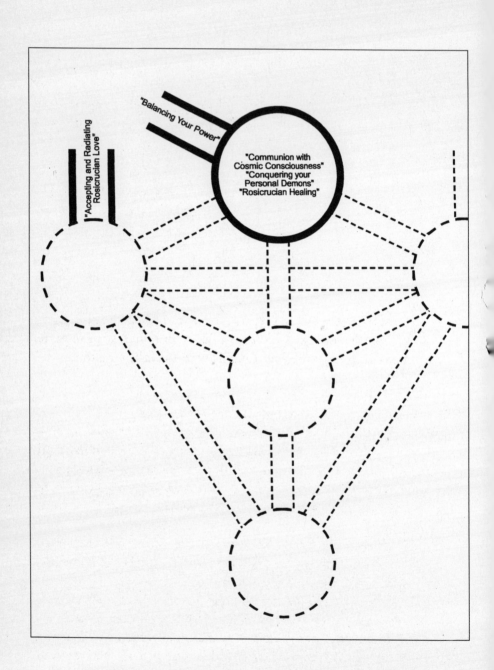

CHAPTER 9
THE ADEPT LEVEL

A t this level, you will prepare for and experience the all-important state of cosmic consciousness. But before you do, it is important to explore yourself thoroughly with the following tool.

CREATING INNER HARMONY

When you are ready to work at the Adept level, you will have all the tools available to you for accomplishing anything you want in life. You will understand the components of all of the elements of your being. It is only necessary that you actively use these tools to create a singular direction in your life. With this tool, you can do just that.

1. Take out your goals. Review them to be certain which ones you have already accomplished and to discover if there are any that you no longer desire.
2. Compare your goals with your values and your beliefs, and compare these with the emotions that you experience.
3. You must now systematically make adjustments to your values, add or remove beliefs and emotions. Use all of the technologies that you have learned. What beliefs do you need to

accomplish your goals? Install them. What emotions may you need to get where you want to go? Create anchors. What painful feelings do you experience that may get in your way? Change them into pleasure. What values and rules do you have that are in conflict with your goals? Adjust them. Work on every part of your life until you are energized and prepared to take consistent action toward your goals.

Once you have created this inner harmony, you will be a thousand times more effective at using all of the magical tools of the New Hermetics and ready to move on to the next tool.

CONSCIOUS COMMUNION WITH COSMIC CONSCIOUSNESS

This tool is really the whole purpose of the New Hermetics. Its intention is to establish a permanent and replicable link between your personal and cosmic consciousness. I discuss this process and the various ways to accomplish it in detail in my book, *21st Century Mage.* I highly recommend that you read this book as a supplement to this tool. Many elements of the New Hermetics and magical practice in general are laid out from a different perspective.

The transcendental experience produced by the following tool is what has been called "illumination." It is a sense of internal knowledge and power produced by a union or connection of your mind with the universal mind. It may take quite a number of repeated uses of this tool, or one of the techniques described in the above referenced book, to achieve a sense of success.

If you have conscientiously explored all of the other tools in this book, then you are ready to use this one. Your results will directly reflect the quality of your previous work. This tool is somewhat different from the previous tools because your conscious mind is incapable of fully producing a "successful" result on its own. This tool requires the cooperation of your unconscious in a very special way. Your unconscious must choose to allow you access to the experience of the totality of yourself. The purpose of all the previous tools has been to shift your consciousness in ways that will facilitate this special experience with your unconscious.

Success with this tool is unmistakable, as it will leave you with an inner knowing that you have experienced yourself in a transcendental way. Really, any of the mystical tools of the New Hermetics may result in your Conscious Communion with Cosmic Consciousness. The following is merely a simple and direct method of soliciting the result by instructing your unconscious with exactly what you wish to experience.

1. Enter the altered state using your meditation anchor (see page 132).
2. Go to your inner temple (see page 90).
3. Perform the New Hermetics grounding and centering if you wish (see page 99), although you can probably omit it at this point if you have really solidified your inner temple with several solid months of work.
4. Face the earth wall of your inner temple. Dissociate yourself from your physical life by saying something to yourself, such as, "I have a body and goals, but I am not my body or my goals. If I were to change or to lose some part of my body or my goals, I would still be me. I am something beyond these things."
5. Face the water wall of your inner temple. Dissociate yourself from your emotional life by saying something to yourself, such as, "I have emotions, but I am not my emotions. If I were to change or to lose some of my emotions, I would still be me. I am something beyond these things."
6. Face the air wall of your inner temple. Dissociate yourself from your mental life by saying something to yourself, such as, "I have thoughts and beliefs, but I am not my thoughts and beliefs. If I were to change or to lose some part of my thoughts and beliefs, I would still be me. I am something beyond these things."
7. Face the fire wall of your inner temple. Dissociate yourself from your values and desires by saying something to yourself, such as, "I have values and desires, but I am not my values and desires. If I were to change or to lose some part of my values and desires, I would still be me. I am something beyond these things."

8. Move up out of your inner temple into the globe of white light above. Feel and see yourself within this white light.

9. Allow yourself to expand effortlessly outward toward the concepts of infiniteness and omnipresence. Feel yourself expanding and dissolving until you feel you are as large as you can be. You may feel a floating sensation or a sense of oceanic awareness.

10. Allow yourself to expand effortlessly outward toward the concepts of all-lovingness and infinite bliss. Feel yourself expanding and dissolving until you feel you are as love-filled as you can be. You may feel a floating sensation or a sense of oceanic awareness.

11. Allow yourself to expand effortlessly outward toward the concept of omniscience. Feel yourself expanding and dissolving until you feel you are as aware as you can be. You may feel a floating sensation or a sense of oceanic awareness.

12. Allow yourself to expand effortlessly outward toward the concept of omnipotence. Feel yourself expanding and dissolving until you feel you are as powerful as you can be. You may feel a floating sensation or a sense of oceanic awareness.

13. Allow yourself to move beyond these sensations into pure undifferentiated white light, feeling yourself at once all things and disintegrating into nothing.

14. Cease being anything and allow yourself to be with infinity.

15. Return to your inner temple.

16. Perform the New Hermetics grounding and centering.

17. Return to normal consciousness.

CONQUERING YOUR DEMONS

We all have sneaky little fearful demons of the mind that creep up on us and prevent us from taking various actions and experiencing life to the fullest. These demons actually have a positive intention—to protect us, save us from pain or rejection, or many other intentions. However, the result of their actions in our unconscious is the inability to take action. You have already seen these demons in action whenever you have "checked in with yourself" while using one of the New Hermetics tools and found yourself doubting or holding back. Unchecked, these demons can prevent us from achieving our dreams, and can keep us from even accomplishing the simplest of our goals. However, these personal demons only have the negative influence that we give to them, and they can be transformed into powerful allies to assist us in our life's transformation.

With this tool, you will be asked to look at some difficult issues, but you will do it in a relaxing and tranquil way. You have now gained the power to establish control over your demons and harness their power. All that you need to do is redirect the power of these disturbing pieces of consciousness with the power of your dawning cosmic awareness, and you will increase your personal effectiveness by staggering proportions. You may need to use this tool a number of times to gain the full benefit of it.

1. Enter the altered state using your meditation anchor (see page 132).
2. Go to your inner temple (see page 90).
3. Perform the New Hermetics grounding and centering (see page 99).
4. Look toward the east of your temple, ahead of you, to the yellow wall of air. See the billowing clouds of yellowish air before you and, as you watch and feel the swirl of air, begin to become aware of your deepest fears about your intellect, education, communication skills, or anything else to do with the mind. These fears often manifest as an inability to draw conclusions or getting stuck in overthinking things. Let all of your fears come to you peacefully, knowing that you will soon be free of them. These fears may come to you as words, or feelings, images, or a combination of these.
5. Visualize all of these fears swirling and coming together in the form of a giant golden yellow demon in the billows of cloud in the east (see figure 50, page 204).
6. Look squarely at this demon and say something to the effect of "I have allowed my thoughts to be influenced by you, but from now on, I will be in charge of my thoughts, and I will use my thoughts to empower me. From now on, I will rule the affairs of my mind. From now on, I will run my brain. I

command you to submit yourself to my power and the power of cosmic consciousness."

7. Extend your imaginary hand toward the demon, and see a ray of light come from your hand, feeling the power of cosmic consciousness flowing through you. As you see this ray come into contact with the demon, visualize it bowing to you in submission and dissolving back into its element.

8. Look to the south of your temple toward your right, the red wall of fire. See burning flames before you, and as you watch and feel the burning of fire, begin to become aware of your deepest fears about your creativity, sexuality, or your will. These may be fears that you are doing things wrong or that what you're doing isn't good enough, or that you are on the wrong path, a sense that you are doing something morally

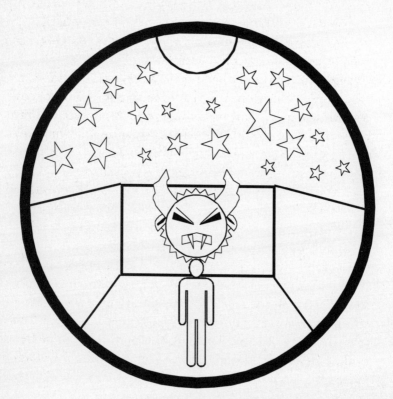

Figure 50. See all of your fears coming together in the shape of a demon.

wrong, or that somebody else may be doing something wrong. Let all of your fears come to you peacefully, knowing that you will soon be free of them. These fears may come to you as words, or feelings, or images, or a combination of these.

9. Visualize all of these fears swirling and coming together in the form of a giant fiery red demon forming in the flames of the south.

10. Look squarely at this demon and say something to the effect of "I have allowed you to influence me with morals and codes that I did not choose. From now on, I will be the master of my values and my beliefs, and I will choose empowering values that free my mind to have the greatest set of choices. I will have true personal power. From now on, I will rule the affairs of my will and passion, and I will control my creativity. I am free to express myself in any way that I choose. I command you to submit yourself to my power and the power of cosmic consciousness."

11. Extend your imaginary hand toward the demon, and see a ray of light come from your hand, feeling the power of cosmic consciousness flowing through you. As you see this ray come into contact with the demon, visualize it bowing to you in submission and dissolving back into its element.

12. Look toward the west of your temple behind you, the blue wall of water. See undulating waves of water before you, and as you watch and feel the waves of water, begin to become aware of your deepest fears about your relationships and emotions. Become aware of any hidden fears about what others think of you, fears about love and friendship and feelings of loneliness, fears about who is in control in your personal and professional relationships, fears about being in charge, fears about not being in charge. Let all of your fears come to you peacefully, knowing that you will soon be free of them. These fears may come to you as words, or feelings, or images, or a combination of these.

13. Visualize all of these fears swirling and coming together in the form of a giant pulsing blue demon forming in the flow of water behind you in the west.

14. Look squarely at this demon and say something to the effect of "I have allowed you to fool me into looking for approval from the outside. I have felt lonely and scared and unloved. In fact, it is I alone who control my emotional state. From now on, I will only look to myself for all questions of behavior, and I will rule my own emotions. I will rule the affairs of my heart. I will experience positive relationships and control over my emotional body. I command you to submit yourself to my power and the power of cosmic consciousness."

15. Extend your imaginary hand toward the demon, and see a ray of light come from your hand, feeling the power of cosmic consciousness flowing through you. As you see this ray come into contact with the demon, visualize it bowing to you in submission and dissolving back into its element.

16. Look toward your left, to the north of your temple, the black wall of earth. See rocky structures forming before you and as you watch and feel the formations of earth, begin to become aware of your deepest fears about your finances and work, your physical body and personal environment. These may be anxieties about money, health, and anything that has to do with the body or the physical well-being, fears about being poor or rich, fears about your personal comfort. Let all of your fears come to you peacefully, knowing that you will soon be free of them. These fears may come to you as words, or feelings, images, or a combination of these.

17. Visualize all of these fears swirling and coming together in the form of a giant earthy black demon forming among the structures in the north.

18. Look squarely at this demon and say something to the effect of "From now on, I will decide consciously what is pleasant and what is unpleasant, and I know that I can make any unpleasant experience into a pleasant one by changing my frame of reference. From now on, I will rule the affairs of

my body. I will have health. From now on, I accept wealth. I will enjoy being in my physical body. I command you to submit yourself to my power and the power of cosmic consciousness."

19. Extend your imaginary hand toward the demon, and see a ray of light come from your hand, feeling the power of cosmic consciousness flowing through you. As you see this ray come into contact with the demon, visualize it bowing to you in submission and dissolving back into its element.
20. Perform the New Hermetics grounding and centering.
21. Return to normal consciousness.

You have now caused your demons to submit themselves before you, and you are in control of your life. You can look at your demons clearly and see that they are now yours to command.

Radiating Rosicrucian Love

The purpose of this tool is to experience a positive feeling toward the universe. This will help you immensely, both in your life with others and in your internal life. You may use this tool as often as you like to forgive and to spread love to the whole world. As you perform this tool, you will be participating in the healing of our planet.

There is, of course, quite another form of Rosicrucian love that will be dealt with in Appendix 4. This present tool is of a more universal character and is wholly safe and positive.

1. Enter the altered state using your meditation anchor (see page 132).
2. Go to your inner temple (see page 90).
3. Perform the New Hermetics grounding and centering (see page 99).
4. Look up at the globe of light above you. Become aware of the crown of your head. Feel a pure white light entering the crown of your head from the shining globe, making your whole head begin to glow. This is the energy of cosmic consciousness moving into your body.

5. Feel and see this light energy moving down to your heart. As it reaches your heart, allow it to turn into golden sunshine and feel a feeling of love as your heart begins to open. Feel the warmth of the universe opening your heart.

6. Think of all the people, plants, and animals that you know very well. Encompass them in the golden light of your heart. Forgive them for everything hurtful they have ever done to you, and know that they are forgiving you on some level. Send them love and happiness and peace.

7. Think of all the people, plants, and animals that you know moderately well. Encompass them in the golden light of your heart. Forgive them for everything hurtful they have ever done to you, and know that they are forgiving you on some level. Send them love and happiness and peace.

8. Think of all the people, plants, and animals in the town where you live. Encompass them in the golden light of your heart. Forgive them for everything hurtful they have ever done to you, and know that they are forgiving you on some level. Send them love and happiness and peace.

9. Think of all the people, plants, and animals in the region where you live. Encompass them in the golden light of your heart. Forgive them for everything hurtful they have ever done to you, and know that they are forgiving you on some level. Send them love and happiness and peace.

10. Think of all the people, plants, and animals in your nation. Encompass them in the golden light of your heart. Forgive them for everything hurtful they have ever done to you, and know that they are forgiving you on some level. Send them love and happiness and peace.

11. Think of all the people, plants, and animals in the world. Encompass them in the golden light of your heart. Forgive them for everything hurtful they have ever done to you, and know that they are forgiving you on some level. Send them love and happiness and peace.

12. Think of all the beings in the universe. Encompass them in the golden light of your heart. Forgive them for everything hurtful they have ever done to you, and know that they are

forgiving you on some level. Send them love and happiness and peace.

13. Return to your inner temple.
14. Perform the New Hermetics grounding and centering.
15. Return to normal consciousness.
16. Use this tool often.

BALANCING YOUR POWER

With this tool, you will move through a series of experiences that prepare you for the ups and downs that life will bring to you. You have now explored all of the essential tools of the New Hermetics. This tool is a benediction and a final conditioning to prepare you for the road ahead.

1. Enter the altered state using your meditation anchor (see page 132).
2. Go to your inner temple (see page 90).
3. Perform the New Hermetics grounding and centering (see page 99).
4. Look up at that shining globe of white brilliance above your head and visualize this globe becoming larger and brighter, descending on you.
5. As the light grows, feel the crown of your head. Feel the pure white light of cosmic consciousness entering the crown of your head so that your whole head begins to glow. This is the energy of cosmic consciousness moving into your body.
6. Feel and see yourself flowing upward into the light of your globe as the light flows into you.
7. Visualize your inner temple below you and be aware that, in your inner temple, you are at the true equilibrium of forces. You are connected to the foundation and the source of your power, and you can experience yourself balanced by the elements on all sides, at one with the forces of the universe. Know that, wherever you are, your inner light and power is with you.

8. Move peacefully forward into the future. When you have troubles and difficulties—whether in relationships with people, financial troubles, or personal confusion—you will really start to connect with these troubles and fully experience the difficulties that everyone faces. Feel, see, and hear these experiences vividly. As you are fully immersed in this, realize that these troubles are opportunities to display your strength, your character, and the force of your will to overcome obstacles. Know that these troubles will offer new learning experiences, and that everyone who has ever accomplished anything has experienced failure and opposition. Know that the greater the obstacles and the trials, the greater the triumph and the glory that is experienced in the long run. From now on, you will look forward to struggles and challenges because you know that only through them will you experience success.

9. Move peacefully forward to a time in the future when you will have great success and victories, whether in wonderful relationships with people, success in your career, or financial abundance. As you really start to connect with your triumphant experiences, fully experience the joy of success. Feel, see, and hear these experiences vividly. As you are fully immersed in this, realize that it is still important for you to maintain your humility, because, although you may have accomplished much, there are those who have accomplished more. Avoid looking down on those who have accomplished less, because you are unaware of the full circumstances of their lives. Your greatest strength is in your humility. Too much pride is the undoing of all great people.

10. Move peacefully forward to another time in the future and experience yourself respecting your body, eating appropriately, and moderating your behavior to keep yourself healthy and strong. Experience yourself maintaining your mental equilibrium; your passions, emotions, and beliefs are under your control. Feel, see, and hear these experiences vividly.

11. Move peacefully forward to another time in the future and experience yourself doing good to others just because it feels

good. This is the only reason to do good. You are acting passionately, thinking rationally, being yourself. Feel, see, and hear these experiences vividly.

12. Perform the New Hermetics grounding and centering.

13. Return to normal consciousness.

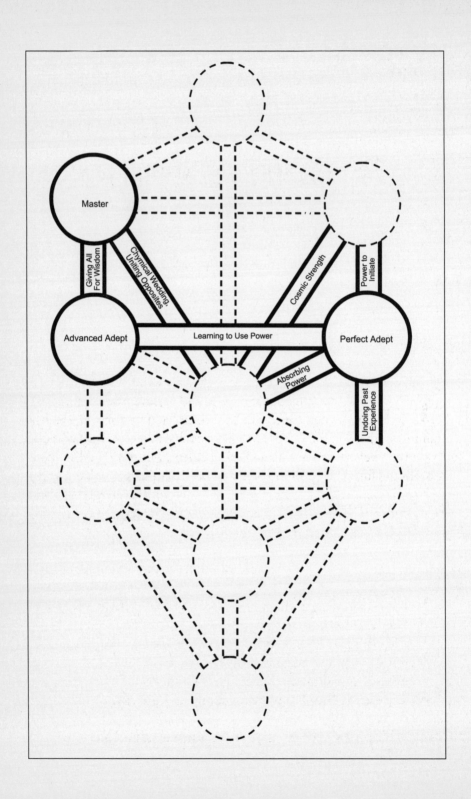

CHAPTER 10

BEYOND ADEPTHOOD

You now have a fairly complete sketch of the New Hermetics, and I wish you strength and speed and perseverance on this, life's greatest journey. Once you have completed the New Hermetics training up through the Adept level, it is possible to receive further training in the levels of Advanced and Perfect Adept. I hope to publish these tools in the future, but, for now, they are only available privately. I will be happy to share these with anyone who has gone through the New Hermetics program in this book and shown some evidence of using these technologies to transform their lives.

Among other things, the Advanced Adept receives training in:

- Problem-solving and perseverance;
- Losing self-importance;
- Undoing past experience;
- Invoking and managing power;
- Evocation and mastery of spiritual forces;
- Influencing people and forces subtly and directly.

Some of the topics in which the Perfect Adept is trained are:

- Attracting and managing prosperity;
- The power of persuasion;
- Human meta-programming;
- Creating instantaneous rapport;
- Removing any last "karmic blocks" that are holding you back;
- Oneness with the universe.

Many of these skills and tools will become self-evident as you continue to work with the tools in this book. I heartily encourage you to practice the tools in this book often, and you will swiftly find yourself confidently striding among the Lords of Light.

BUILDING A PHYSICAL TEMPLE

There are those in the world who enjoy both the artistic and symbolic expression afforded by building a physical temple, filled with ritual implements, magical circles, and various other accoutrements. If you are one of these people, you can still benefit from the New Hermetics. You can easily convert the patterns of mental and spiritual direction that you find in the New Hermetics tools into physical rituals performed in a physical temple. In fact, it may be very useful for many people to do this.

If you would like to do this, I suggest acquiring or making a magick pantacle (circular disk), cup, sword, wand, and lamp. The pantacle should be a round disk made of wax, wood, or gold, engraved with a symbol you feel represents the universe for you. You can just engrave it with a pentagram, a hexagram, or the seal of the New Hermetics if you wish (see front cover). The cup should be made of silver. The sword should not be so big that it overwhelms the other implements. All of the objects should be harmonious in size. The wand can be a cylinder of copper or wood, preferably cut from a tree and prepared lovingly by you. The lamp can be any sort of light, candle, oil burning lamp, etc.

You can then use these articles in each of the levels respectively. For instance, you can incorporate or simply hold onto the pantacle during rituals of the Initiate level. The cup can be incorporated into tools for the Zealot level, etc. You can find some other ideas about ritual movement in the Appendices.

HAVING TROUBLE?

If you are having trouble using any of the tools in this book, please review the instructions carefully. Any problems that you may have will almost certainly occur because you are missing one or more of the instructions. Ask yourself these questions, although these are obviously quite subjective:

- Are you getting properly into the altered state of consciousness?
- Are you vividly imagining the components of the exercises (you don't have see things in crystal-clear detail, but you must be really *into* it), or are you just muddily fantasizing?
- Are you immersed in your visions? In other words, are you seeing your inner temple in the first person, or are you looking at yourself from the outside? It is vital to your success to be "in" your visions, except in those cases where it says otherwise in the instructions.
- Are you involving all parts of yourself in these tools? Are you physically, emotionally, mentally, and spiritually involved?

If you are doing all of these things and still having trouble with any parts of the New Hermetics, then by all means, please try something else. Try anything else. These tools are designed to meet the basic needs of most people, but you are an individual. At all times, trust your own creativity and make the New Hermetics your own. Feel free to modify any components of these tools to make them most effective for you. Only you can know exactly what's right for your spiritual journey. The most important thing is to keep going, and make sure you're always having fun.

You may also wish to add or change words, symbols, or concepts to help you feel connected with your own belief systems throughout this program. Please feel free. You may eventually find yourself limited if you change things to fit one rigid set of beliefs, but you should still do it if it makes you happy. It is your life and your inner world. You will find the correct way for you to proceed in all things inside of yourself. That is ultimately the goal. This book is merely a guide to help you get in touch with yourself as deeply as possible. Strive on!

Love is the law, love under will.

Appendix 1

A Note to the Studious Qabalist
on Errors Found in this Volume

Some of the information in this manual may appear to fly in the face of some conventional "orthodox" Hermetic and Qabalistic teachings. For instance, I have placed the Cup of water in Yesod and the Sword of air in Hod. The reason behind this particular switch is that the cup is a collecting tool, and the sword, a dissecting tool. These images have, in my experience, fit archetypically more appropriately in the spaces to which I have assigned them. Quite simply, the cup is an emotional tool, and the sword, an intellectual tool. The reason for the original placement was so that the Golden Dawn grades would correspond with the elements in the order of Tetragrammaton. In practical occultism, however, the tools (and their archetypal equivalents, the emotions and the mind) are used much more commonly in the positions in which I have placed them.

The cup is lunar in nature and corresponds quite swimmingly with the lotuses of the seven chakras. The sword is a weapon, man-made, and corresponds quite naturally with the intellectual qualities of Hod. It is said that air and water share many qualities and transform one into the other. This is represented in astrology by the fact that Aquarius (the water bearer) is an air sign, and Scorpio (whose highest symbol is the eagle) is a water sign. At any rate, my choice was based entirely on the practicalities of synthesizing a number of divergent streams into a sensible whole. The tools work. You may feel free to make any philosophical adjustments you find necessary along the way.

This is equally true of the many other Qabalistic "faux pas" that the diligent reader may discover. I wrote this note purely with the intent of relieving the steam that may be building up in the heads of any of you scholars out there. Yes, not everything that is contained in this book is pure Qabala, or pure anything else. It is a functional system that will help you reach your greatest potential, and that is what I consider important. In order to create an "archetypal consistency," it was necessary for me to adjust certain relationships, images, and correspondences so that information was consistent, both with itself and with my own practical experiences exploring the subtle planes beyond the physical. I take full responsibility for any error that you notice; what's more, I probably made the errors intentionally. If you notice errors, omissions, generalizations, or distortions of your personal belief system, please feel free to write them down. This will make you feel much better. I'll be glad to look them over if you send them to me, but I will probably not have time to reply. I do enjoy feedback of any kind.

APPENDIX 2
Scientific Illuminism Omissions

Quite a bit of the material in *The New Hermetics* is adapted from the Scientific Illuminism practices of the A∴A∴.However, there are a few notable omissions. In this appendix, I will reference the titles of specific documents, all of which can be found in *The Equinox*, volumes 1 to 10. If you are unfamiliar with these documents, the following won't make much sense and you can safely skip it. If you are familiar with these instructions, you are probably wondering why some of them aren't found in the New Hermetics. I'll briefly explain why they haven't been addressed in these pages.

Liber AL, The Book of the Law
The statements made in the present book are wholly in accord with my own personal take on the law of the new aeon, but I have consciously and specifically made no attempt to convert anyone to any philosophy other than their own self-discovery in this manual.

Liber NV and Liber HAD
These works specifically deal with the mystical exploration of the *Book of the Law*. While I find them interesting and personally meaningful, far too much explanatory material would have been necessary for them to be incorporated practically into the simple scheme of the New Hermetics. They are fairly simple and straightforward. If there is sufficient interest in them, I may in the future create a specifically Thelemic set of New Hermetics tools. Since they are, however, so simple and to the point, there is probably little I could add. I have created an alternate

course for studying the New Hermetics tools specifically related to the degree work of Ordo Templi Orientis. It would be inappropriate to share this course publicly, but I would be happy to provide it to initiates of the order, along with my thoughts about the above-mentioned documents.

LIBER ASTARTE

This is an elegant and useful instruction, but it did not find its way into the scheme of the New Hermetics largely due to the instructions of my "inner planes contacts." I originally had a simplified version of it in the works, but I was specifically told to leave it out because the theme of this work is "Know Thyself," and the instructions of *Liber Astarte* might tend to blur self and a limited image of godhead into a potentially confusing morass. I do think it is a valuable practice. I also feel that it is a very straightforward and simple instruction, and I could probably add little to it. In many ways, the path of love is one of the most effective and powerful methods of attainment and certainly deserves your attention.

LIBER JUGORUM

I have had a problem with this instruction for quite a while, certainly since I experimented with it personally. The problem with this instruction is quite simple. Frater Perdurabo compares speech, action, and thought to various animals, and then suggests that you train these animals with physical abuse. We have long since ceased to train animals with this kind of negative reinforcement, and it seems terribly foolish to inflict this sort of abuse on yourself. Animals and our own minds respond much more quickly and effectively to positive instruction and rewards than to punishment and threats. Also, as Emile Coue pointed out nearly one hundred years ago, when the imagination and the will fight one another, the imagination always wins. Therefore, I suggest you concentrate on developing your imagination, for it is with this organ that you will discover your true will. Why waste time trying not to think of a blue elephant when you can spend that same time creating a joyous connection with the source of all?

LIBER RESH

While I think this practice may be very useful, it did not find its way into these pages for reasons similar to those that led me to omit *Liber Astarte*, as well as the fact that it is rather sectarian in character, referencing Egyptian gods that could be unfamiliar and potentially confusing. It is also fairly complete in and of itself, and there's little I could add other than simply pasting it in. If it seems like a valuable practice to you, I suggest that you incorporate it into your life. It is certainly congruent with the present work. See especially the section on conscious action, which will give you some indication of my feelings on the matter.

LIBER YOD AND LIBER OS ABYSMI

These and a few of the other excluded instructions are advanced and not necessary within the frame of this volume.

LIBER SAMEKH

See Appendix 5 in this volume.

APPENDIX 3
Movement and the
New Hermetics

Several of the tools of the New Hermetics have asked you to conduct some sort of movement in their practice; however, this is such an important subject that I wanted to add a few extra notes. Because this book has so much stressed the mental, the importance of the physical may have been lost. The physical is really of utmost importance, because you are one organism—physical, spiritual, emotional. It is all one. If you ignore any parts of this whole, you will not get to the totality of the greater you. Here are a few more ideas about using physical expression to understand and work with yourself.

MOVEMENT TO CHANGE STATE

When we are feeling miserable, we often seem to get stuck. Even if we know how to get out of the miserable state—such as using one of the techniques in the section of this book on emotion—sometimes we can't even get ourselves to do that. We sit huddled in our misery. This is usually because we are trying to prevent some acutely bad feeling from coming upon us by holding ourselves motionless in a dull pain.

But this is the worst thing we can do because, by freezing up and staying still, we hold onto the negative energy and inhibit the flow of vitality. If we stay in this state for too long, a doctor will come along and tell us that we are depressed and start prescribing all sorts of mind-altering substances, which by then we will probably require just to feel somewhat normal. This is all unnecessary. There is a simple remedy to feeling down, tired, sad, angry, depressed, frightened, panicky, unloved, hateful, hated, and a million other negative feelings. That solution is movement.

Any kind of movement will begin the process—taking a walk, exercising, dancing, somersaulting, or even jumping. It is only necessary to start, and the movement itself will do much of the healing. Emotions need to move. If you are still, they get stuck. This is true both spiritually and physically. Many toxins move through the lymph system, which only works properly when we are active and taking full respirations. When we are motionless, we are sitting in our own toxicity. When we move, our whole metabolic system cranks into gear, and we become healthier and more vibrant. Once you begin moving, the technologies in the emotion section of the Zealot level will really begin to flower.

MOVING TO EXPLORE ENERGIES

You can also move to explore the different kinds of energies that we've been working with, and even to discover new energies. This topic is so rich and important that I am working on a book about it right now with the woman who taught me how significant movement can really be. However, here are a few suggestions based on some of the work that we have already done in the New Hermetics. Try these different kinds of movement, and I guarantee that you will understand these energies in a much more dynamic and intimate way than ever before. You will understand these forces with your whole being, and their transformative power will exponentially increase.

Fire

As you move experiencing the element of fire, let the motions of your whole body be passionate, vigorous, wild, destructive and creative, dynamic and powerful. Feel the heat and the dryness of fire, the expansion and consumption. Feel the fire and let yourself discover your unique experience of fire.

Water

As you move experiencing the element of water, sway your body rhythmically in sensual, undulatory movements. Feel the cool flow of water, the dance, and discover what water is to you.

Air

As you move experiencing the element of air, feel the lightness all around you and within you, delicate and ephemeral, ever-changing, insubstantial, discovering your own unique relationship with air.

Earth

As you move experiencing the element of earth, feel the heaviness and solidity, the slowness and the strength, the patience and the endurance of earth, and your own experience will grow.

You can also experience this with the gods, the alchemical principles, the paths and sephiroth on the Tree of Life, the chakras, and anything else you can imagine. Simply use your imagination; the tools and ideas you have learned in this book will create the opening, letting your own experience guide you as you move along. Movement is so immediately powerful that it cannot fail to affect and transform you. You may wish to use movement significantly in the middle of other work to create a framework for your efforts.

NEW HERMETICS BREATH AND MOVEMENT EXERCISE

Another way that you can use movement beneficially is to combine it with the breath. The Chinese have many excellent techniques that fall under the general heading of *chi gong*. If the ancient magicians had a similar system, it has been lost to us. Certainly they were aware of the importance of both movement and breath.

I have combined the elemental grade signs from the Golden Dawn with some simple chi gong-type movements and created a simple breathing and movement sequence that is in perfect alignment with the work we have been conducting.

Earth

As you do the earth breath and movement, please get in touch with the energy of earth. Feel the heaviness, hardness, and solidity of the element. Become aware of the solidity of your body, your weight and structure. Experience the sensations of stability, composure, and calmness moving up into your body, strengthening you and growing the powers of earth within you.

1. Stand with legs shoulder-width apart, knees slightly bent, arms at your sides, your hips, head, and shoulders relaxed.
2. Inhale, raising your arms slowly until they approximate a forty-five degree angle above your shoulders. As you are inhaling, draw earth energy up into your body from below your feet (see figure 51, below).
3. Exhale, lowering your arms, letting them continue to move back behind you to a comfortable position. This is one breath. Repeat as many times as you like.

Water

As you do the water breath and movement, please get in touch with the energy of water. Feel the moisture, the wetness of water; feel its cool flow. Feel the rhythmic flow of the water in your body, your blood, your tears, your sweat, and your saliva. Experience the cool flow of water moving up through your body, cleansing you and flowing out through the top of your head, leaving the powers of water as it cleanses away all negativity.

Figure 51. Moving and breathing in the earth element.

1. Stand with your legs shoulder-width apart, knees slightly
   bent, your hips, head, and shoulders relaxed. Hold your
   hands in the shape of a downward-pointing triangle over
   your belly, your thumbs and forefingers touching.
2. Inhale, slowly raising your arms straight up over your head.
   As you are inhaling, draw water energy up into your body
   from below your feet, moving it up through the top of your
   head (see figure 52, below).
3. Exhale, lowering your arms down the sides of your body,
   sending the water energy showering down around you. This
   is one breath. Repeat as many times as you like.

Air

As you do the air breath and movement, please get in touch with the
energy of air. Feel the lightness, the rushing speed of air whirling through
you, blowing out old ideas. Feel the air filling your lungs, and the energy
of the air moving through your whole body, charging you with the
powers of air.

1. Stand with your legs shoulder-width apart, knees slightly
   bent, arms at sides with hands facing away from your body,
   your hips, head, and shoulders relaxed.

Figure 52. Moving and breathing in the water element.

2. Inhale, raising your arms with hands upward along the sides of your body, holding your hands above you as if you were supporting the sky. Imagine that you are gathering air as you raise your arms (see figure 53, below).

3. Exhale, lowering your arms in front of your body, pushing the gust of gathered air through your being, clearing you of old and outworn beliefs, making room for new knowledge. This is one breath. Repeat as many times as you like.

Fire

As you do the fire breath and movement, please get in touch with the energy of fire. Feel the strength and vigor of fire bursting through you, feel the heat of your body and the power of your life energy. Feel the force of fire moving through you, expanding out into the world.

1. Stand with your legs shoulder-width apart, knees slightly bent. Keeping head and shoulders relaxed, hold your hands in front of your face in the shape of an upward-pointing triangle, your thumbs and forefingers touching.

2. Inhale, holding your hands in the triangle as you fill yourself with fiery energy from above (see figure 54, page 228).

Figure 53. Moving and breathing in the air element.

3. Exhale, pushing your arms forward and outward to the sides in a sweeping circle, imagining the force of fire moving outward as your will expressed passionately into the world. Bring your hands back to the triangle as you inhale. This is one breath. Repeat as many times as you like.

Spirit

For spirit breath, simply stand relaxed, tranquil, breathing fully, feeling the movement of currents through your body. These may be quite profound if you have done the previous breath patterns a number of times each.

There are several other Hermetic Order of the Golden Dawn gestures that could be developed into breathing exercises, such as the sign of the enterer and of silence, the rending and closing of the veil, the LVX signs, and the NOX signs. These are not necessary for the level at which we are currently working, and I won't describe them in detail, but the advanced student will certainly be able to put them to some good use in this way.

Figure 54. Moving and breathing in the fire element.

Appendix 4
New Hermetics Sex Magick

Sex magick does not form an official part of the New Hermetics instructions, but it is an important and useful technique for the adept, and I thought I should address it in some way. A lot of wordy drivel has been written on this subject in the last few years. In truth, sex magick is very simple and straightforward and can be entirely explained in just a few sentences.

Sex magick has often been thought of as an unsavory and sometimes evil technique, relegated to the "left-hand path" or "black magick" side of a number of magical and mystical traditions. However, this is not at all true. The idea that sex magick is evil came from the antiquated and malignant idea that women were, in and of themselves, somehow impure. Hence any connection with them was viewed as necessarily partaking of evil. We are now capable of recognizing the absurdity of this.

Sex magick is a beautiful sacrament, an ecstatic communion with a lover. Through this connection, you can achieve communion with the cosmic consciousness of the universe. When a woman and a man come together in the act of love, they are, at that time, the true image of the living god, male-female, mother-father, Pangenetor-Pangenetrix. (However, it should be noted that sex magick can, for the most part, be performed by any other combination of partners, male-male, female-female, or even by oneself—with varied results, of course).

To really understand sex magick, you must consciously recognize that, in our genital fluids, there is the power to create life—millions of lives, in the case of the male of the species. The moment of orgasm is a moment of pure potentiality in which a new life can be created. This power can be directed toward making a baby or, as in the case of sex magick, any other creation. In the sex act, we are connecting the spiritual and physical planes in a singular fashion, and we can direct this spiritual power in any way imaginable. Usually, this takes the form of a specific "bud-will," or desired manifestation in the sex magician's lives. This can be anything from wishing for increased wealth to connecting with some form of godhead. Really, any purpose can be adapted to a sex-magical context. However, this technique should only be used, if at all, once you have explored and mastered all of the previous techniques of the New Hermetics. It requires a one-pointed concentration that will be quite natural once you have completed the New Hermetics program through the Adept level. That being said, here is a general outline of the procedure.

1. A purpose must be decided in advance of the sex act. For what will this sexual act be consecrated? It is a good idea for manifestations to have some sort of talisman, which should be handy at the time of the operation. Those described earlier in the text are perfectly suited to this purpose. For other purposes, you may easily adapt many of the earlier techniques in this manual (i.e., gods, elementals, energies, etc.) All people involved with the sex act should definitely be working toward the same purpose.

2. Participants should bathe, consciously purifying themselves, clearing body and mind for the upcoming rite.

3. Before commencing, some sort of preparatory exercises should be undertaken, such as entering the altered state (see page 73) and perhaps performing the New Hermetics grounding and centering (see page 99). But at this point in your career, your inner world should be naturally balanced enough that a few simple focusing breaths may suffice. You may also wish to perform some sort of opening ritual. This is up to you.

4. Sexual stimulation can now begin. For the moment, the purpose of the rite should be forgotten so that the fires of passion can really be ignited. Sexual stimulation should be complete and passionate. Once all is ready sexually, you can begin having sex.

5. Once you start having sex, your concentration must turn back to the purpose of your operation and remain directed toward that purpose for the rest of the rite. Direct your pas-

sion ecstatically toward the purpose of the operation. If working with a partner, truly connect with your partner on all levels and, through that connection, direct your will.

6. This passion must extend for as long as possible, no less than half an hour. Passion should be heaped upon passion, until orgasm seems impossible to avoid. However, do not yield to orgasm. Instead, continue focusing on your purpose, directing it through the ecstatic connection with your partner. It may be useful to chant some sort of mantra or spell to keep you directed. This mantra can be anything from the name of some god to a word of power or some rhyming couplet you write or borrow. You can also use one or more of the New Hermetics tools during this period if it seems applicable. Continue until you lose all sense of yourself and your partner in pure ecstasy.

7. Orgasm should be simultaneous with your partner, if you have a partner. This indicates both your intimate connection and the singularity of the act. At the moment of orgasm, the will must be entirely focused on the operation, even though consciousness may be lost in ecstasy.

8. The sexual fluids should be gathered. A portion of them should be placed on the talisman if there is one, and the practitioners should consume the rest. This is of the utmost importance and must not be omitted. These fluids are the charged product of the working; this is a true Eucharist. The combined fluids of man and woman are a perfect substance, "not living and not dead, neither liquid nor solid, neither hot nor cold, neither male nor female."[10] It is one substance, containing all possibilities. This is the Elixir of Life.

It is said that, once a person begins to use sex magick, all sexual acts must be consecrated toward magick, or negative energy may accumulate due to the unbalanced forces attracted by undirected sexual force. I have not necessarily found this to be true, but I think it best to share this information in the interest of prudence and completeness.

APPENDIX 5
The Bornless Ritual

Since the publication of my previous book, *21st Century Mage* (Weiser Books, 2002), which is all about obtaining cosmic consciousness or the Holy Guardian Angel, many people have asked me about The Bornless Ritual, which was the tool that Aleister Crowley used to attain to his own Holy Guardian Angel.[11] I was initially hesitant to include anything on this subject, because it is a very specific rather than a universal tool. However, I have since found quite a lot of value in it, using the "barbarous words" as a sort of long, varying mantra. Some may find this a useful tool. Still, it is not without trepidation that I add this as an appendix to the New Hermetics system as an alternate or complementary technique for attaining cosmic consciousness.

With this mental ritual, you will expand yourself actively into cosmic consciousness. The purpose is to establish an active link between your consciousness and cosmic consciousness. This link will increase your power to transform your life positively. This method is similar in structure to the New Hermetics grounding and centering pattern, but adding some ancient magical words of power from the Hellenistic Hermetic formulae of ancient Alexandria. The magick words that you will use with this are at least 2000 years old. There seems to be a mysterious power that comes with age. It will, of course, take some time to memorize all these formulae. I personally made a CD to guide me through the whole process. You may wish to do the same, or you can purchase my CD if you like.[12] The technique goes as follows:

1. Enter the altered state using your meditation anchor (see page 132).
2. Go to your inner temple (see page 90).

3. Perform the New Hermetics grounding and centering if you wish (see page 99), although you can probably omit it at this point if you have really solidified your inner temple with several solid months of work.
4. Look up at that shining globe of white brilliance above your head, and you can allow this globe to become larger and brighter.
5. Become aware of the crown of your head. Feel the pure white light of cosmic consciousness entering the crown of your head so that you see your whole head beginning to glow. This is the energy of cosmic consciousness moving into your body. Feel and see this light energy moving through you, feeling the warmth and tingling of pure pleasure and joy as ecstatic waves of energy wash over you. As you experience the pure pleasure of the light of cosmic consciousness filling your being, say to yourself:

I invoke you Bornless One, beingness that
has no beginning and no end.
You who create the earth and the heavens.
You who create the night and the day.
You who create the darkness and the light.
You are myself made perfect that no one has ever seen.
You are matter, destroying to create, you are force,
destroying to create.
You have distinguished the just and the unjust,
the female and the male.
You produce the seed and the fruit,
making all to love and to hate one another.
You create the moist and the dry and that
which nourishes all life.
I am your prophet to whom you have given your mysteries.
Hear me, for I am yours. You are myself made perfect.

6. Now look toward the east of your temple ahead of you, to the yellow wall of air. See billowing clouds of yellowish air before you, and see a giant golden yellow being forming in

the billows of cloud in the east, a bird, perhaps. This is the guardian of the element of air. Move into the wall, becoming one with the guardian, feeling the awesome elemental power of the guardian within you, glowing brightly. Allow yourself to expand outward to fill the universe more and more with each word as you say to yourself the sacred words:

AR . . . THI-A-O . . . RHE-I-BET . . . A-THE-LE-BER-SET . . . A . . . BE-LA-THA . . . AB-E-U . . . EB-E-U . . . PHI . . . THE-TA-SO-E . . . IB . . . THI-A-O

7. Say to yourself:

Hear my word, and make all spirits subject to my command, so that every spirit, whether of the heavens or of the air, of the earth or beneath the earth, on land or in the waters, and every force, feeling, and form in the cosmos is mine to command.

8. Look toward the south of your temple toward your right, the red wall of fire. See burning flames before you, and see a giant fiery-red being forming in the flames of the south, a lion, perhaps. This is your guardian of the element of fire. Move into the wall, becoming one with the guardian, feeling the awesome elemental power of the guardian within you glowing brightly. Allow yourself to expand outward to fill the universe more and more with each word as you say to yourself the sacred words:

AR-O-GO-GO-RU-BRA-O . . . SO-TO-U . . . MU-DO-RI-O . . . PHA-LAR-TA-O . . . O-O-O . . . A-PE

9. Say to yourself:

Hear my word, and make all spirits subject to my command, so that every spirit, whether of the heavens or of the air, of the earth or beneath the earth, on land or in the waters, and every force, feeling, and form in the cosmos is mine to command.

10. Look toward your right, to the west of your temple behind you, the blue wall of water. See undulating waves of water before you, and see a giant pulsing blue being forming in the flow of water behind you in the west, a dragon or serpent, perhaps. This is the guardian of the element of water. Move into the wall, becoming one with the guardian, feeling the awesome elemental power of the guardian within you glowing brightly. Allow yourself to expand outward to fill the universe more and more with each word as you say to yourself the sacred words:

RU-A-BRA-I-A-O . . . MRI-O-DOM . . . BA-BA-LON-BAL-BIN-A-BAFT . . . A-SAL-ON-A-I . . . A-PHE-NI-A-O . . . I . . . PHO-TETH . . . A-BRA-SAX . . . A-E-O-O-U . . . I-SCHU-RE

11. Say to yourself:

Hear my word, and make all spirits subject to my command, so that every spirit, whether of the heavens or of the air, of the earth or beneath the earth, on land or in the waters, and every force, feeling, and form in the cosmos is mine to command.

12. Look toward your right, to the north of your temple, the black wall of earth. See rocky structures forming before you, and see a giant earthy black being forming among the structures in the north, a hippopotamus or cow, perhaps. This is the guardian of the element of earth. Move into the wall, becoming one with the guardian, feeling the awesome elemental power of the guardian within you glowing brightly. Allow yourself to expand to fill the universe more and more with each word as you say to yourself the sacred words:

MA . . . BAR-RI-O . . . I-O-EL . . . KO-THA . . . A-THO-RE-BA-LO . . . A-BRA-OT

13. Say to yourself:

*Hear my word, and make all spirits subject to my command, so
that every spirit, whether of the heavens or of the air, of the
earth or beneath the earth, on land or in the waters, and every
force, feeling, and form in the cosmos is mine to command.*

14. You will now connect more fully with cosmic consciousness,
so look up once again at that shining globe of white brilliance above your head and allow this globe to become larger
and brighter.
15. As the light grows, you become aware of the crown of your
head. Feel and see the pure white light of cosmic consciousness entering the crown of your head so that your whole
head begins to glow as the energy of cosmic consciousness
moves into your body.
16. Allow yourself to flow upward into the light of this globe as
the light flows into you, and feel yourself grow upward and
outward, dissolving into the light as you say to yourself the
sacred words:

*A-OT . . . A-BA-OT . . . BA-SA-U-M . . . I-SAK . . .
SA-BA-O . . . I-A-O*

*This is the ruler of the universe whom the winds fear . . .
This is who made voice and all things were created.
Ruler, master, helper . . .*

*I-E-O-U . . . PUR . . . I-O-U . . . PUR . . . I-A-OTH . . . I-
A-E-O . . . I-O-O-U . . . A-BRA-SAX . . . SA-BRI-AM . . . O-
O . . . U-U . . . E-U . . . O-O . . . U-U . . . A-DO-NA-I . . .
E-DE . . . E-DU . . . AN-GE-LO-STON-THE-ON . . . AN-
LA-LA . . . LA-I . . . GA-I-A . . . A-E-PE . . . DI-A-THAR-
NA . . . THO-RON*

I am the bornless one.
Having sight in the feet: strong and the immortal fire.
I am the truth.
I am the one in lightning and in thunder.
My sweat is the rain that showers the earth with life.
My mouth is ever flaming.
I am the maker and begetter of the light!
I am the grace of the world.
The heart girt with a serpent is my name.

I-A-O . . . SA-BA-O

17. Allow yourself to move beyond these sensations into pure undifferentiated white light, feeling yourself at once all things and disintegrating into nothing.
18. Cease being anything and allow yourself to be with infinity.
19. Return to your inner temple.
20. Perform the New Hermetics grounding and centering.
21. Return to normal consciousness.

Bibliography and
Suggested Reading List

HERMETICS

Bardon, Franz. *Initiation into Hermetics.*Wuppertal, Germany: Ruggeberg-Verlag, 1993.

Flowers, Stephen. *Hermetic Magic.* York Beach, ME: Samuel Weiser Books, 1995.

Mead, G.R.S. *Thrice Great Hermes: Studies in Hellenistic Theosophy and Gnosis*, Volume II. London: Theosophical Publishing Society, 1906.

Three Initiates. *The Kybalion.* Chicago: Yogi Publication Society, 1940.

MAGICK AND OTHER ESOTERIC TECHNOLOGY

Carroll, Peter. *Liber Kaos.*York Beach, ME: Samuel Weiser Books, 1992.

—————-. *Liber Null and Psychonaut.* York Beach, ME: Samuel Weiser Books, 1987.

Crowley, Aleister. *The Equinox*, Vols. 1-10. York Beach, ME: Samuel Weiser Books, 1999.

—————-. *Magick Liber ABA.* York Beach, ME: Samuel Weiser Books, 1998.

DuQuette, Lon Milo. *The Magick of Thelema.* York Beach, ME: Samuel Weiser Books, 1993.

—————-. *Enochian Sex Magick.* Phoenix, AZ: New Falcon Publications, 1991.

Gawain, Shakti. *Creative Visualization.* New York: Bantam Books, 1978.

Hine, Phil. *Condensed Chaos.* Tempe, AZ: New Falcon Publications, 1995.

Kraig, Donald Michael. *Modern Magick.* St. Paul, MN: Llewellyn Books, 1992.

Mathers, S. L. Macgregor. *The Book of the Sacred Magic of Abramelin the Mage.* New York: Dover Publications, 1975.

Nema. *Maat Magick.* York Beach, ME: Samuel Weiser Books, 1995.

Newcomb, Jason Augustus. *21st Century Mage.* Boston, MA: Weiser Books, 2002.

Regardie, Israel. *The Golden Dawn.* St. Paul, MN: Llewellyn Books, 1989.

—————-. *The One-Year Manual.* York Beach, ME: Samuel Weiser Books, 1990.

————. *The Tree of Life*. York Beach, ME: Samuel Weiser Books, 1972.
Silva, Jose. *The Silva Mind Control Method,* New York: Pocket Books, 1977.
Starhawk. *The Spiral Dance*. New York: Harper and Row, 1989.
Steinbrecher, Edwin. *The Inner Guide Meditation*. York Beach, ME: Samuel Weiser Books, 1988.

NLP

Bandler, Richard and John Grinder. *Frogs into Princes*. Moab, UT: Real People Press, 1981.
————. *The Structure of Magic*. Palo Alto, CA: Science and Behavior Books, 1975.
————. *The Structure of Magic 2*. Palo Alto, CA: Science and Behavior Books, 1976.
Robbins, Anthony. *Unlimited Power*. New York: Ballantine Books, 1986.

PSYCHOLOGICAL MODELS

Jung, Carl G. *Alchemical Studies*. Princeton, NJ: Princeton University Press, 1967.
————. *The Archetypes and the Collective Unconscious*. Princeton, NJ: Princeton University Press, 1969.
Leary, Timothy. *Game of Life*. Tempe, AZ: New Falcon Publications, 1995.
Reich, Wilhelm. *The Function of the Orgasm*. New York: Farrar, Strauss and Giroux, 1973.
Wilson, Robert Anton. *Prometheus Rising*. Phoenix, AZ: Falcon Press, 1983.

QABALA

Crowley, Aleister. *777 and other Qabalistic Writings*. York Beach, ME: Samuel Weiser Books, 1973.
Fortune, Dion. *The Mystical Qabala*. York Beach, ME: Samuel Weiser Books, 1984.
Regardie, Israel. *A Garden of Pomegranates*. St. Paul, MN: Llewellyn Books, 1988.
Wang, Robert. *Qabalistic Tarot*. York Beach, ME: Samuel Weiser Books, 1987.

Notes

1   Manly P. Hall, *Lost Keys of Freemasonry* (Richmond, VA: Macoy, 1968), p. 96.
2   Manly P. Hall, *Lost Keys*, p. 96.
3   Redintegration is an archaic word meaning "restoration to a former state."
4   *The Book of Thoth* by The Master Therion (Aleister Crowley). A Short Essay on the Tarot of the Egyptians. (London: O.T.O., 1944. *The Equinox*, III (5). Reprinted York Beach, ME: Samuel Weiser, 1992), p. 89.
5   G. R. S. Mead, *Thrice Great Hermes, Book II* (York Beach, ME: Samuel Weiser, 2001), p. 127.
6   See also Aleister Crowley, "The Soldier and the Hunchback ! and ?," *The Equinox* Vols. 1–10 (York Beach, ME: Samuel Weiser Books, 1999), p. 111.
7   See also Aleister Crowley, "The Herb Dangerous II: The Psychology of Hashish," *The Equinox*, Vols. 1–10 (York Beach, ME: Samuel Weiser Books, 1999), p. 57.
8   See Robert Wang, *Qabalistic Tarot* (York Beach, ME: Samuel Weiser Books, 1987).
9   See also Aleister Crowley, "Liber O: VI," *The Equinox*, Vols. 1–10 (York Beach, ME: Samuel Weiser Books, 1999), p. 18.
10 Aleister Crowley, *Magick Liber ABA* (York Beach, ME: Samuel Weiser Books, 1998), p. 267.
11 See also Aleister Crowley, "Liber Samekh" in *Magic Liber ABA* (York Beach, ME: Samuel Weiser, 1987), pp. 513–41 and Stephen Flowers, "The Rise of the Headless One" in *Hermetic Magic* (York Beach, ME: Samuel Weiser, 1995), pp. 182–84.
12 Available at my online store—*http://store.vendio.com/centerofchanges*.